SMALL TALK

How to Start a Conversation & Talk to Anyone

(How Simple Training Can Help You Connect Effortlessly With Anyone)

Caitlin Smith

Published By Regina Loviusher

Caitlin Smith

All Rights Reserved

Small Talk: How to Start a Conversation & Talk to Anyone (How Simple Training Can Help You Connect Effortlessly With Anyone)

ISBN 978-1-77485-323-8

All rights reserved. No part of this guide may be reproduced in any form without permission in writing from the publisher except in the case of brief quotations embodied in critical articles or reviews.

Legal & Disclaimer

The information contained in this book is not designed to replace or take the place of any form of medicine or professional medical advice. The information in this book has been provided for educational and entertainment purposes only.

The information contained in this book has been compiled from sources deemed reliable, and it is accurate to the best of the Author's knowledge; however, the Author cannot guarantee its accuracy and validity and cannot be held liable for any errors or omissions. Changes are periodically made to this book. You must consult your doctor or get professional medical advice before using any of the suggested remedies, techniques, or information in this book.

Upon using the information contained in this book, you agree to hold harmless the Author from and against any damages, costs, and expenses, including any legal fees potentially resulting from the application of any of the information provided by this guide. This disclaimer applies to any damages or injury caused by the use and application, whether directly or indirectly, of any advice or information presented, whether for breach of contract, tort, negligence, personal injury, criminal intent, or under any other cause of action.

You agree to accept all risks of using the information presented inside this book. You need to consult a professional medical practitioner in order to ensure you are both able and healthy enough to participate in this program.

TABLE OF CONTENTS

INTRODUCTION 1

CHAPTER 1: BEGINNING OF SMALL TALK 3

CHAPTER 2: TOP PLACES TO UNLEASH YOUR SMALL TALK SKILLS 11

CHAPTER 3: GIVE PEOPLE A CHANCE HOW TO BE A GOOD LISTENER? 20

CHAPTER 4: PLACING AN END TO AWKWARD SILENCE 30

CHAPTER 5: TALKING AS AN IMPORTANT LIFE SKILL 37

CHAPTER 6: SPECIAL TIPS FOR THE SHY 43

CHAPTER 7: CONFIDENCE, AND SELF-ESTEEM 53

CHAPTER 8: TIPS TO BEGIN A CONVERSATION 58

CHAPTER 9: INNOVATIVE METHODS TO START SMALL TALKS 79

CHAPTER 10: TIPS TO MANAGE A TENSE CONVERSATION 87

CHAPTER 11: EVERYTHING TO DO WITH BEING PRESENT 92

CHAPTER 12: BUILDING A CAREER AND BUSINESS USING SMALL TALK 98

CHAPTER 13: SMALL TALK STARTERS 104

CHAPTER 14: SMALL TALK STARTER GUIDE 117

CHAPTER 15: ENDING CONVERSATION 127

CHAPTER 16: EFFECTIVE SMALL TALK BEGINS WITH CONFIDENCE 132

CHAPTER 17: APPLYING SMALL TALK TO YOUR ADVANTAGE.. 150

CHAPTER 18: LISTENING WITH CARE 156

CHAPTER 19: TAKE THE PLUNGE..................................... 161

CHAPTER 20: THE OPENINGS THAT ARE SUITABLE FOR PEOPLE WHO ARE SHY 170

CHAPTER 21: DISPLAY GENUINE INTEREST 177

CONCLUSION.. 185

Introduction

Small talk is much more crucial than you realize. It is easy to think you don't need it since it's just about minor things, but it is a major influence on the various aspects that you live in. It actually serves as the basis of the everyday lives of a lot of people, not only in their personal lives as well as in their professional lives.

Small talk sessions are beneficial in that they are a great way to create a pleasant atmosphere in different settings. For workplaces For instance, you could utilize it prior to when a formal meeting commences, creating an atmosphere that is more relaxed. Maybe, you want to discuss with your colleague the morning commute or weather.

The advantage of doing this is that it lets you to establish a connection with others. It lets them know that you're eager to listen to their thoughts and that you're willing to engage with them. It's also a option for introverts, specifically people who are uncomfortable in social situations to get noticed.

By using this book, you'll be able to get the attention of most, if not all of the people who are around you , by creating the impression that you're interested in the things they've got to share. It can help them feel more relaxed through small discussions.

Chapter 1: Beginning of Small Talk

Small talk is too intimate and big talk seems too massive.
- Anna Quindlen
Strangers who meet in the very first conversation typically begin conversations by engaging in small conversation. This chapter offers ideas and guidelines to design conversations that are small-talk at the beginning of.
The preparation for Small Talk
Before you can start small talk there are ways to prepare yourself for the conversation. A little preparation can make the difference between an enjoyable conversation that is low-risk and a uncomfortable exchange. For small talk, it is important to prepare avoid distractions and lessen anxiety.
The absence of distractions can increase the chances of engaging in small-talk. Put away electronic devices, including cell phones. Don't wear headphones.When you are at home, switch off the TV and the computer screens. In a way, by minimizing

distractions, conversational partners will be more likely to observe each other's conversationsal cues.

The idea of engaging in conversations with strangers could cause people to feel nervous. As per psychotherapist Dr. Thomas A. Richards Social anxiety is among the three most prevalent mental health issues within the United States. People who talk to strangers should make efforts to reduce the anxiety level of their friends.

Always remind you that your possible conversation partner is also uncertain. Keep in mind that the theory of uncertainty reduction suggests that people acquire information through conversations that help to reduce their uncertainties regarding each other. The act of starting small talk might seem intimidating at first, but when the conversation progresses the two parties involved in small talk get more comfortable with one another and consequently, more comfortable. In addition, think about the fact the fact that conversation, as a rule is low-risk.

To reduce anxiety further Psychologists recommend a mix of visualization and breathing exercises. Take an inhale while holding it for a couple of seconds, then exhaling. Concentrate on the sensations of breath that is coming through your nasal passages. Humboldt State University psychologist Brian A. McElwain promotes this breathing technique, frequently including it in the group of mindfulness is led by him. When they focus on their breath the participants can take their focus and away from distracting conversations in their heads.

Psychologists also suggest visualization exercises. The psychotherapist Dr. Cathryne Maciolek suggests individuals can utilize visualization exercises to manage anxiety and to perform better all day. Visualize yourself engaging in a relaxing low-risk conversation with your potential conversation partner. Research has shown that if you are able to visualize yourself performing something you're more likely to accomplish it effectively.

The world goes by quickly however taking just a few minutes to do some exercises such as visualization and breathing can result in a dramatic and visible difference in your anxiety levels. If you are in a positive mental state you can make small talk much more enjoyable for you.

Engaging in Small Talk

A lot of conversations start with small conversations. Small talk is a way to have parties and conversations that are a secure form of conversation. Consider small talk as being the "feeling out" part that occurs during conversations. Small talk starts with three steps: locating and creating an experience that is shared, sharing information that is related to that sharing experience and, finally asking a question related to that experience. Communication expert Dr. Carol Fleming refers to these steps as anchoring inspiring, and revealing.

To start small-talk, you must first think of an experience you can share with your potential conversation with your partner. Students share with the teacher. People who share the same street are in the same weather. The audience members of a concert are able to share their experiences of attending the event. When you next are in the same room as at most one other person think of three fascinating experiences you are able to share with the other people in the room. The environment you are in is likely to have an array of experiences that everyone present.

After being identified, you can you can make a comment, or even a remark about the experience you shared. For instance, imagine that a professor just given a stimulating talk to his students. A student in the class named Brett might tell his fellow classmate, Amanda, "Professor Gus is extremely clever." In this moment, Brett has identified and identified a shared experience is shared with Amanda the instructor.

In the event that Amanda is a positive response, Brett should continue into the conversation, sharing details about himself in relation to the instructor. Brett might say, "I feel like I do not have enough time to take part in the class." In this instance, Brett exposes some aspect of himself. Through relating in the context of the common experience Brett provides Amanda something that she can relate to.

In the end, Brett should ask an open-ended inquiry about the teacher. Brett could ask "How would you rate the forthcoming exam?" This question encourages Amanda to continue the conversation. Brett must listen to Amanda's answer with a keen eye. At this moment, Brett has successfully initiated small conversations with one of her classmates.

Communicators begin small conversations by identifying and commenting on an experience shared and sharing relevant information about themselves, and then asking an open-ended and relevant question. Make sure you and your partner in the same experience, share your personal characteristics and then encourage your partner to share their thoughts. The Dr. Fleming teaches these steps with an acronym A.R.E. : anchor, reveal, encourage.

Once started Small talk can be carried on in a myriad of directions. A large part of the fun of small-talk is its unpredictable nature. Therefore, it will not be feasible to give readers word-for-word scripts that ensure the success of small talk. Indeed, scripts that are memorized can hinder people from fully engaging their guests when they attempt to recall the appropriate words to use. The next chapter contains specific tips to aid readers in becoming skilled small talkers. Examples of how to apply them to real-world situations accompany these guidelines.

Chapter Summary

Remove or disable electronic devices that could interfere with the conversation.

Make use of breathing exercises and visualization to lessen anxiety over small conversation.

Begin small talk by discovery of, and investigation into, an experience shared by the two.

Keep in mind A.R.E. : Anchor, reveal, encourage.

Chapter 2: Top places to unleash your Small Talk Skills

Location, location, location! This is only half the fight. If you're planning to meet someone, you have to know where you can meet them. It is also important to establish a reason of why you want to meet and why you'd like to get in touch with them. When you've got that clear the purpose, you can pick an appropriate location where you can meet with the individual that you are seeking. There are a lot of occasions where people attend events for networking, or attend a certain place in the hope that of "meeting anyone," without any details or details. That's why specificity is worth millions of dollars. If you know exactly what you're seeking, you can be able to save hours (days and months, or years) of hassle and time. We only have a limited amount of time, make the most of it.
Locations for Meetings:
Coffee Shop:

Coffee shops are a popular place for a relaxing time, to have a chat with people who are new to them and, of course, have a few drinks. It is free to chat with anyone new in the coffee shops for three reasons:

They'll be more open to new ideas because of the relaxed setting.

They're eager to connect with them, because if they weren't, they'd be at home.

It's an easy place to get used to meeting amazing strangers.

The next time you're at a coffee place and you are there, try chatting with a stranger just to have fun and discover where it leads you.

Grocery Store

If you're looking to make acquaintances in a store or other store, you likely enjoy food, are concerned about your health or are looking an individual to make dinner. This is a great spot to begin conversations and receive great recommendations for food from other customers.

Laundromat

It's simple to talk with your L-mat. In the beginning, you'll be waiting for a long period of time as the soap is washed out of every one of your clothes and why not talk to each other for a while? It'll make the process go much quicker too.

Gym

If you're at the gym, you're aware that those who go there for three reasons: they wish to remain healthy and in form, are looking to shed weight, or gain some muscle and become strong. Being motivated by the same reasons of going for a workout is a fantastic method to create a sense of commonality. Of course , the best method to begin an exchange at a gym is to solicit the "spot," or advice about how to build muscle. But, when you go to the gym, you'll see that a lot of individuals wear business clothing, such as the business they work for or for the school they attended or even a military-themed shirt, which all offer excellent conversation starters.

The Street

In large cities it is an ideal location to meet a diverse number of people. It is possible to have 25 new conversations in just 2 or 3 hours. It's a fantastic opportunity to expand your perspective on how fascinating the world is, and how it's composed of so diverse nationalities and cultures - only to discover that even though we may appear to be different, we are not.

School

It is a simple and easy venue to meet people because you are likely to see them at a minimum of a few times throughout the week. It can be difficult in the event that you bring romance into the picture due to fact that you'll see them often.

Meet with your neighbors in the seat to learn more about what they're about and what they are doing to have fun. If you see anyone walking around that appears interesting or you're interested about, just say "Hi," and ask your question in the context of the emotion you're experiencing. For instance, "I'm a little nervous when I meet you, because I don't usually talk with strangers. I'd like to ...(ask your question (which you are curious about).)."

Or "I'm curiousabout how you love the Dodgers and you're in Florida."

If you enjoy them Invite them to participate in something that you both enjoy. Simple right?

Adult Sports Leagues

Sports are among the best ways to meet friendships. Both of you are dedicated to having fun and being active on the fields. So why not look for other hobbies and leave the field and have fun elsewhere?

The Mall

If you're in the market for to the mall, or you need advice...the shopping mall can be the ideal spot to go. Women especially like to be part of the men's fashion quest and some guys enjoy shopping as well. The best method to start conversations in a shopping center is to ask, "Hey can I get your opinion in a short time. Which one do you prefer better (hold your shirt in place A) and (hold up shirt B))?"

At this point, you are able to decide if you would like to carry on the conversation or and not (based on the option you or your partner picks). Have fun.

Concerts

The atmosphere of concerts is a blast. While they can be noisy however, they can also be fantastic opportunities to make new acquaintances, particularly outdoor events in which you are able to meet someone and begin a conversations.

Bar

The drinks are flowing as people become more relaxed, relaxed even drunk. The atmosphere is becoming more social, and the volume continues to increase each hour. Because the people feel more comfortable, it's easier to get to know people, so long as you're okay with noisy people and the music. Take a look because it's fun and you could be able to meet a fascinating person or two.

Volunteering

If you're a volunteer with a big heart, and the person sitting next to you probably has too. It's an amazing way to meet someone with similar interests. From trying to do something positive by helping people who are less fortunate out, or just helping out your community.

If you're capable take the opportunity to chat with customers (of of course, only if you're not too busy or you do not have to do with work). It's a great opportunity to get comfortable and make the best utilization of the time you have. In addition, you could be the next person you meet or someone who will provide you with a fun time.

Church

Similar to volunteering, you'll find an interest that is based on your religious beliefs. Perhaps you're just interested and want to learn more about your religion or you're an avid churchgoer. Whatever it is, it's an ideal place to say "Hi and how do you feel?" introduce yourself, and then begin to use the Small Talk Method.

Meetup Group

Thank God for the Internet...and Meetup. If you've not been aware of Meetup and I'm not sure where you've hidden in the last 10 years. If you've never explored www.meetup.com it's time to. It's a great way to meet people who share your interests. What is a better method to meet new friends than through activities you enjoy?

Book (or Film) Club

People like reading. Others prefer to watch films. This is a great method to meet new people with similar interests.

At Work

Chat with your colleagues. It's as simple as that. You can say "hi" to someone who is walking by and discover who your coworker (or building or building) is. Maybe he'll be your future best man for your wedding. Perhaps they are someone you'll eventually need as a business associate Perhaps he will be able to watch your kids (or pet) this weekend. You never know! It is only possible to gain from taking part in this discussion and learning about other people.

Airplane

The fact that the requirement to sit with another passenger on an airplane, this is ideal for having conversations. If you're in that situation, take out the "conversation container" and take a look. Check out the person close to you. You might get to know someone who could give tickets for backstage access to an upcoming Rolling Stones concert, or someone who has a spare room at his home located in Copenhagen, Denmark.

17. Hotel

If you're staying in the hotel, you can talk to staff and guests. In the majority of Hotels (and hostels) there's an open lobby where guests are able to gather and have a small talk.You can chat freely in the lobby, and even order coffee or food. It's a great opportunity to begin conversations with a friend, and you might even be able to make a new acquaintance.

Chapter 3: Give People A Chance How To Be a Good Listener?

In the world of human nature, listening well is vital. We can make assumptions too fast, even when we consider an individual, and we usually categorize them in accordance with our prejudice. If the way we label to someone is negative, we instantly reduce our attention and go in our shells. No matter what they declare, we don't pay attention to them any more, instead, we look for a reason to leave.

The most frequent misconception we are plagued with is the that we are unique, and therefore believe that there's no one else who thinks the same way as we do. Unfortunately, the more time we spend in solitude, inside our enclosed cocoons in our cocoons, the more difficult becomes to believe there are others in the world Earth that think in the same way. In addition even more, the more people who are unable to comprehend us and the more we think that nobody else will ever know us.

We often feel misunderstood as we are convinced that we won't meet people we can discuss our thoughts with. We then think to ourselves, what's the purpose of going out to meet strangers? If we already believe it's not worth the effort or that it's impossible to meet.

I was similar to this. As an introvert, living in a deep-seated complexity within many about my ideas, opinions,, and internal struggles could not be shared or understood by other people. Through the years I have discovered that there's a need to be able to open yourself up and give others the chance to see through our facade and understand our innermost thoughts and feelings.

Being vulnerable doesn't necessarily suggest that you must reveal all or any information about your life. What I'm trying to convey here is that vulnerability sometimes implies showing the interest of others in their conversation , before they reciprocate by showing an interest in you too.

How do I accomplish this?

In general, introverts tend to be great listeners. The main advantage that this natural trait gives us is our capacity to effortlessly pay focus on what others are speaking. It is also crucial to remember that listening to others can be extremely demanding on our energy. This means that we should not listen to every and all information people are able to throw at us. We must be selective and create filters and discover how to be smart listeners.

While listening is a lot easier for introverts, those who are more outgoing should be taught to become intelligent listeners.

The smart listener is someone who can determine the quality of the information they are exposed to by asking the most pertinent questions. They attempt to comprehend the motives behind people's actions, their root motivations, and the real meaning behind their words. They become involved in their fellow's stories and are able to identify what motivates them.

To do this, it is essential to know how to ask the correct and relevant questions. These are open-ended questions that require the listener to just answer with yes or no. They will have to dig deeper into details, give you some background information or paint an image verbally.

A case study of how this technique can be used to enhance the casual presentation is shown below.

"I lived in London. It was an enjoyable time", Alex said.

"Cool Did you like it?", Arina asked.

The question is negative question due to the fact that it is non-intentional and closed-ended. It is clear that Arina doesn't really want to dig into the deeper issues and comprehend Alex's motivations and motives. However, Alex may interpret this as Arina asking the question to show that she is courteous. Therefore, the most likely response Arina may get is:

"Yeah I went to London. London was beautiful and had lots of things to do", Alex replies.

Did this story tell Arina any information about Alex specifically? No. It did not provide her with any relevant details. In the absence of a proper structure, Arina will most probably think that Alex is boring. Inability to ask the correct question didn't create an occasion for him to talk about his feelings.

An example of a great example of a good

"I lived in London. It was an enjoyable time", Alex said.

"Cool What did you enjoy in London?", Arina asked.

"London is a city with an amazing ambience that is found only in this part of the world. The possibility of it combining the fascinating exterior with its bustling work culture is amazing to me. Furthermore, due to my raucous personality, I can easily become tired of small cities as I am a fan of a spontaneous lifestyle. That's why London offer me the opportunity to push myself beyond my limits to keep up with the many individuals rushing for their source satisfaction", Alex answers.

This type of interesting inquiry that Alex asked can't be addressed by "Yea it's great". Arina's query gives Alex the chance to talk about and discuss his favorite things about London.

Did her query provide her with more details? Yes it did. If she was on the seeking a acquaintance who would enjoy living in or visiting smaller cities, she could easily eliminate Alex out of her list and then gracefully end the conversation. If she doesn't, she could delve into more details about his attraction for big buzzing cities like London.

In light of the fact that Alex excels in fast-paced environments, it's reasonable to conclude that he could be an executive or have an extremely demanding job. Perhaps he's highly motivated, high-flier, or and an overachiever. But he could also be a bit of a liar. To know more about this intriguingly charming guy, Arina can now choose from a variety of questions that

check or confirm her beliefs. The questions she choose to ask will be determined by what draws her about the man. The types of questions she can inquire about include:
What was your home before you relocated to London?

If you're talking about the fast-paced life and the fast-paced lifestyle, how do you think it is best personal or professionally?

What keeps you engaged and focused in London?

This kind of question shows that Arina is, in the worst instance, at least a little curious about Alex without explicitly stating the fact.

The trick to asking these kinds of queries is have others talk to you while you're listening intently which makes them feel like you're an extrovert. In addition, because you're receiving a lot more information than you're providing, you will be able to decide whether you think an individual intriguing or not. Another aspect to consider in these meetings is that the majority of people love talking about themselves, and that in most cases, people will only talk about their positive experiences with you. In these gatherings, keep in mind that the majority of people want to find people who are a good listener as friends. Bravo to you for listening is among the most enjoyable tasks for introverts such as us.

After all is completed, any judgment you make about a person or incident from your interactions and conversations will be more logical and dependable as compared to the conclusion from your preconceived notions or a stereotype.

For introverts, small conversations are usually viewed as an unnecessary insignificant amount of time. However we can be scared when those we've recently had the pleasure of meeting (acquaintances) have to share personal stories or experience during our first encounter. First of all, we're usually not interested in this kind of nonsense. To make matters worse we are easily anxious. Therefore, we try to avoid these scenarios, and we only accept the former to occur when we trust the person, thereby demonstrating our vulnerability.

What can be done to make even small conversations less annoying?

One of the first points to make contact with an introvert who is involved in a conversation that is not planned is to be in control of the situation. We, as introverts, need to take the route of least resistance. Because we can exhaust our energy when we try to be both listening and speaking so we should be aware of the decisions we make in conversations. It is also true that the most efficient and of the least investment for those who are introverts is to listen. We often see ourselves as natural listeners.

Being in control of any conversation is about knowing and knowing how to ask correct questions so that you are able to steer the conversation according to your preferences. If you are not looking to engage in a casual conversation, make sure you ask the right questions. If asking the right questions doesn't work, then end the conversation. If someone else is asking you questions that become becoming more personal, it suggests that they're interested in your story. It also suggests that you must begin asking the right questions If you are interested in their business.

Being introverted, you will be best to let others to open to you before you begin opening to them. This lets you know and are aware of what they like and what makes them tick, and decide if they're worth your time and time prior to making any commitment to the relationship.

In the end, this strategy will be able to accomplish two birds with one stone, provided that it is executed properly.

Chapter 4: Placing an End To Awkward Silence

If there's a single factor that deters people from engaging in an exchange, it's the possibility of experiencing awkward silence.A majority of people prefer to be by their own company rather than engage in conversations in fear of they'll end up with awkward silence.

What's the best way to deal with awkward silence? Maybe ask questions? In a certain sense however, ask questions in improperly and you could come out as a stalker or even worse, a reporter! This is why it's crucial to not just make inquiries to get them answered. Asking questions helps you build relationships and connect with the person you're talking to emotionally.

It's important to realize that people are naturally drawn objects that appeal to them. Be it experiences, locations or even other individuals, they react better to things that have some kind of connection. That's why it's crucial be aware of how you can ask questions to bring them closer to you. The most effective method to get someone to open up is to ask them questions about the things they are most interested in.

Does this mean you should ask them what their personal interests are right immediately? It's not so much. You must establish the basics of a relationship before you can start asking questions about your personal life.

According to research there is no one particular method to build rapport.Most of it relies on intuition. It's about establishing an understanding or bond between two individuals. It is important to connect with the person you're talking to and make them react to what you are talking about. Do you want to know how you can be to be in tune with someone who you only met recently? Here are a few tips to help you establish rapport with people quickly.

Keep your faith in the positive

Be positive and upbeat. It's impossible to establish relationships with people when you're consumed by negative thoughts. It's not only uncomfortable, but it makes interacting with others more difficult. Imagine having to talk to one who doesn't do anything, just complain. The natural reaction is to turn the other way. That's why you need to take the initiative to bring positivity and energy to any conversation. If you appear friendly and easygoing and friendly, people are more likely to like the way you present yourself. While you cannot be positive every single day the best thing that you could do is to keep the negativity of your down low when you're meeting new people for the first time.

Remember names

Another method of building relationships is to be able to recall names. While it's as easy as it may be, remembering names could be a major influence on people you've only have met. If you can remember and include the name of a person when you speak to them you've already put in an effort acquainted with them better.Make sure you incorporate it in conversations as you think appropriate.

Be careful not to go overboard but you don't want to make the person think that you're mocking them. Recalling the name of a new acquaintance and using it to convey an impression that you were concerned enough to think about the person.

Be sure to match their style of communication

You can also establish trust with someone else by observing their style of communication. Each of us has our individual methods of communicating. There are those who are more verbal in their communication and there are those who are more concerned with non-verbal signals. When you look at how a person communicates, you'll be able mirror their style of communication. Mirroring is a key element to build rapport since it helps establish a sense of familiarity. It's possible that you haven't considered it before however, try to observe your behavior when you're with people you are drawn to. You're more likely to follow the actions of that person because you subconsciously want them to feel connected with you.

Listen actively

You won't be a great communicator if you don't understand how to actively listen. When you're engaging in conversation with anyone, ensure that you're listening actively. Active listening means you pay attention to and take note of the words that someone else is talking about. I'm aware that many people have difficulty paying attention to what other people are saying, because they're focused on their own thoughts. Engaging in listening will force you to place your attention on the person you're speaking to. It is important to reach the point that you're not worried about what you're saying to the person you're talking to, but more interested in what they have to say. The great thing about actively listening is that you'll never be short of things to say since you'll be so engaged in the moment when there will always be a follow-up query to inquire about.

Respect your differences

If you aren't the same way in certain areas, make it an effort to respect the opinions of your fellow citizens. Don't be frustrated by the differing views Instead, view the situation as an opportunity discover more about the person you are talking to. It is important to be aware that communication, as a relationship, requires lots of flexibility to compromise. There is no need to be a winner during the conversation. If you are tempted to be a winner by expressing your viewpoint I would suggest you quit the discussion. There is nothing good that can result from trying to convince others of your opinion particularly when the person you are talking to believes strongly in the beliefs they believe in. The best way to deal with this is to respectfully agree to disagree. Sometimes, just acknowledging of your disagreements will suffice. It is not necessary to make a fuss about it.

Don't be afraid

It's much more complicated than it is But a few adjustments to your posture will assist you in building rapport with everyone you meet. How? by smiling, standing or standing straight. Even when you're not feeling the way you want to you can try to fake it. This is when playing it safe can aid you. If you are meeting people in the beginning, be sure you present yourself in a relaxed and pleasant manner. You'll not only look more confident, but also feel more confident about yourself.

Chapter 5: Talking As An Important Life Skill

It would be extremely difficult to live a life and not be in a position to communicate with people because it is through this that we feel completely. Talking is among the most routine things we do, and we don't always recognize its value, so they never think about it in a serious manner. Talking is essential to all people because it promotes general wellbeing and health. It is an effective way to stay away from stress and anxiety and keeps your heart and mind at ease.

Different people are different. There are people who enjoy talking, and others who prefer not to talk as too much. It is crucial to realize that talking can benefit everyone , and helps relieve stress and tension. It is therefore worth the effort to express the thoughts, emotions, and emotions by talking. Through talking we are able to establish and keep contact with others, which is true for business partners, colleagues families, friends and family. Below are the reasons that talking is considered vital particularly for personal growth:

Decision Making

There are times when we reach the point when we're in a impasse when it comes to making choices. If you're not certain which path is most suitable or advantageous, then speaking with people can be a great help. It lets you explore various perspectives on certain things and will put you in an ideal position to weigh your choices. If you're the type of person who enjoys having conversations with others, I'm certain you'll be a problem navigating through your life. There is a reason that people have different opinions about specific things, and the more you talk to people, with people, the more information you acquire and can make informed choices. It is essentially the study of other people's circumstances and experiences.

Reduce Stress

Stress is thought to be a common health issue that, should be treated as a serious condition can have severe negative consequences. The thing is that it comes from within us, and could eventually take control of every aspect of our lives. It is your responsibility to act and discover every way to deal with it. This is the first step to start by engaging in the social aspect of your life. When I speak about your social life, I also refer to the fact that you have to be more social. According to research, you can relieve yourself of a lot of inner anxiety by talking with people more. This is because when you talk to others they always have the ability to lift your spirits, and they may provide solutions to whatever is troubling you. It is difficult to get through the day when you've hidden so much pain and anxiety within your. Engaging with others can be a great way to get rid of these feelings and helps in getting your mind off of it and putting you back in the present.

Overcome Boredom

Talking can also be an excellent way to pass the time. It is more enjoyable than other activity for leisure. It is the way humans can interact with each other, and through talking, you permit you to develop. This creates a sense of inner peace that helps to relax your body and mind. It is difficult to think about how fast time is while you're out with your family and friends. This is precisely what you need to avoid boredom and enjoying their time in most effectively.

Accurate Information

Another benefit of speaking is that it gives the opportunity to expand your knowledge , which eventually results in improved capabilities. It is certain that when you interact with a variety of people with a variety of thoughts, you'll discover a wealth of information. There are all kinds of discussions that occur and there gives you the chance to listen to what others can say on particular elements or things. If you are more knowledgeable, it will be a sign that you are opening your eyes to new possibilities in your life.

Live in the present

An effective method to forget the past, forget regrets and hurts, and not be worried regarding the future by participating in discussions. It is because if your focus is on participating in specific discussions that means you'll be in the present moment. Another benefit is that you can live a greater satisfaction in your life and be able to conquer anxiety. Talking to others will allow you to be more connected to your life, and of others.

Establish Relations

This is among the main benefits of speaking and is the goal that most of us are trying to attain. Positive relationships develop from people's ability to communicate each other. If you're not able to communicate by sharing ideas and thoughts, it's difficult to progress. It's through having a conversation with someone that you meet them and get to know them better. Once you have that, you'll be more inclined to get in contact with them more often.

Find Solutions

Another reason is that one is able to move forward by figuring out solutions to some of their issues by talking. People you talk to probably have experienced some events or heard about them that they have experienced and may share their experiences with you about the situation you're experiencing. A good source of advice is your family and friends, and only through talking to them.

Enhances confidence

The more you speak to people, the more you boost confidence as well as self-esteem. This is due to the fact that you'll become comfortable speaking up in large groups. Being social is when that your social skills grow and you feel more comfortable in speaking to others and will result in a greater confidence. Fear and anxiety which was once there will start diminishing from time-to-time and you will also begin to value your self, resulting in a higher self-esteem.

Chapter 6: Special tips for the shy

"The violets that grow in the mountains have broken through the rocks."
Tennessee Williams.
(This phrase from his play Camino Real, is on his headstone.)
If you're a shy person, who is not extremely sensitive or introverted and just plain shy, the suggestions above could be quite daunting. The most important thing to remember is accept the fact that you are shy and understand that you're in great company of nearly 48 percent of people who believe themselves shy. Don't be a snarky prick about it and make the most of the advantages it offers you. You're aware of your an excellent ability to listen; you seem non-threatening, maybe even modest, and thus are accessible. You appear more sensitive and empathetic than the majority of people. Perhaps you are perceived by some as mysterious and intelligent? You're certainly more confident than other people. It is important to think ahead before you do

anything and can create an uplifting effect during a stressful time.

If you're facing an event that requires just a little talking skills, there are particular things that can help you.

Make sure you know who is going to be there find out the background of some of them , and also the event - go to the venue prior to the event even if you do not know about it.

In my previous list, I do not recommend committing anything to memory. However, If you're feeling anxious you might want to consider it recommended to work out a concise, solid answer to "How are youdoing?" which is more detailed rather than "Fine". Create a brief but intriguing in-depth, informative and flexible response to "What is your work?" or "Where do you work?" as well.

BREATHE

Do not turn down invitations, but be sure to ensure you are able to make it a part of your schedule. No matter if you're female or male. Make sure your hair looks good and you're satisfied with the look you're wearing.

Be early. Make use of social reconnaissance. Get some drinks and take the time to observe who's at the party the place where the action takes place and where the loners are and the location where the host is, as well as if there's someone you know there. Do you know if there are photographers or reporters in attendance? Where are the restrooms?

If you're requested to appear in the picture...SMILE and say "YES" AND ENSURE they spell your name correctly. (PS .a Hidden device within this text will inform me if you say "No" so I can locate you!)

BREATHE

Create a button with the words: "I AM NOT REALLY SHY. I'm just looking over the prey I am hunting." Wear it.

It's okay to sit in the middle of a group , and pay attention to what's being discussed. SMILE. If you have the chance to join in the conversation, make sure you do it with grace.

You should have an open-ended question to discuss if your natural lull has turned into the sound of a loud silence. "What keeps you busy outside of work?" or "Are you perhaps interested in art/gardening/amateur theatre/ singing in a choir?"

If you're approaching an unfamiliar person, open your mind the memories of the confidence you felt in that moment.

BREATHE

Always be the person who will keep the conversation from any argument.

Be sure to make the most of what you excel at...your ability to communicate and your listening skills.

There are many opportunities to practice your small talks outside of the social events you don't like. Try it out with people in the position of serving you. It is not permitted to behave rudely to begin with for bank tellers receptionists, forecourt workers, receptionists beggars, as well as your local library. If you're able to spare the time you can work as a volunteer for one of the numerous organisations that make use of these types of services. It's much more easy to speak to people with needs that are more urgent than your personal needs. Empathy is among the several skills...make your shyness work for you by giving a warm word to other people.

It's hard work. Not for the faint of heart. The shy and the withdrawn feel that they are not accepted by the social norms which favors the self-confident, assertive, outward-oriented individualist. Certain people develop an image of loneliness and display an image of superiority "I do not need "youness"." Do not fall into this trap.

SPECIALTIPSFORTHEINTROVERT

"Isn't it amazing to realize that the thing that is naturally to you is your strongest strength? Your strength lies in the way you are. It might not seem like a important that you could devote hours to something you are interested in, but the person next door who is extrovert doesn't know how you accomplish it."

Laurie A. Helgoe. Introvert Power: Why Your Inner Life Is Your Hidden Strength

If you're an introvert, at the very least you're more in control of the issue than your timid colleague. This implies that you are able to do something about it. It is likely that you find it difficult to believe that so much importance is attached to the pleasures of social interaction. It's possible you'll be unable acceptance of that "way the way things happen" and become as a constant loner and socially marginalized. That is your choice, however I would like to suggest that changing the entire "small conversation" affair into a game is much more enjoyable. There are certain traits that provide you with an advantage. Let's take a look. You are likely to are above average in IQ and are able to handle a large amount of information in an event. You make your choices carefully and you are able to pay attention to details quickly.

However, even with these strengths you're still not happy and possibly scared of the social setting which requires small conversations. I hope that the tips listed below will be helpful to you.

Pay close focus on your body language. Do not take your cozy cocoon of peace with you. Be tall and relaxed with your shoulders. Don't be a fugitive in the corners. Stand in the center in the space. It is easier to carry things off of moving trays here too! Do not look angry and turn off your mobile phone and not in silent mode.
One thing that introverts do share with shy people is their inward-looking behavior may give the impression they're "stuck-up" or believe they are superior and do not have time to engage in such nonsense as social courtesy. Therefore, look at yourself from an outside perspective. Are you displaying your body's posture as: "I would like to chat with you or I would like to talk with me?"
Create a game to see if you are able to complete the entire game without using your phone as an prop. Bet you can't!
Keep in mind that your brain's neurotransmitters are firing "withdrawal" triggers. This can cause you to avoid eye contact. This is why you need to counteract it. Make sure you keep eye

contact to counteract your slower rate of vocal response.

Any topic that comes up discuss your experiences of the subject instead of the topic itself.

Do not be afraid to speak about the odd details of your experiences. If you feel confident enough, you could even make a few inappropriate remarks. Remember that you are playing the game!

It's okay to not be perfect.

Utilize your natural ability to process details to keep what people tell you. It's a fantastic way to introduce yourself to say "Hello. Tell me how you had the job that you had been looking for with Universal?" Even if they didn't , you've shown one of the main factors in successful small talk and that is an curiosity about the person you are talking to.

Don't evaluate a book based on its cover.

Don't get too excited and exhausted. Learn about the event If you are able. Decide when and for how long you'll attend the event. This is crucial when you are trying to manage small talk in a way that will improve your chances of being promoted and standing in the social scene.

You can give yourself a short "time-out" to escape the noise. Use the bathroom. Go into the garden. If you're in the crowd for a long period of time you could even get in your vehicle for a five minutes of relaxation in the back of your car.

One thing that's the most challenging for you as an introvert is that you prefer to take your time before you make a decision. This is why the person who is more extrovert who typically is quick in their response time, doesn't realize that you're in the "ok let me consider the issue" area, then carries into the conversation. Maybe you can consider using phrases like "I'd need to think about it" or "I have never thought about it this way" as a tactic to hold the conversation to boost your response speed and keep the attention. You can also keep your gaze while showing your face with an "I I am trying to think" look on the face.

In actuality, the entire matter of introversion, shyness and extrovertivity is an arc and the majority of individuals are actually considered to be ambiverts. i.e. people who have both.

Chapter 7: Confidence, and Self-Esteem

If you're looking to live a happier life, it is vital that you start living your life with assurance and self-esteem. This is believed to greatly help an individual's personal development and growth. If you feel confident and have confidence in themselves, it means that they are ready to take chances and open themselves to the world. This opens the door to new possibilities and opportunities in your daily life. It also will make you more innovative.

In addition, speaking is a powerful technique that one can employ to increase their confidence. This is because you'll be better prepared to take on the world and all its difficulties. With confidence, you won't be worried or feel any anxiety when confronting various life events. This is exactly what you need to be able to achieve fulfillment and true happiness.

In terms of self-esteem, you should think of the voice in your head that continuously reminds you of your value. When you have a high self-esteem, it's an inner voice that informs that they are worthy and that they have everything necessary to achieve their dreams and goals become a reality. This indicates that you greatly regard yourself and are able to tackle any obstacle with enthusiasm and confidence. While self-confidence and self-esteem are essential throughout our lives, many people aren't able to attain confidence levels that are high. Below are some of the strategies that can aid you in being more confident and possessing confidence in yourself:

Positive thinking and having a an optimistic attitude toward life will make you more confident and confident.

Learning more about yourself and believing in your potential and abilities helps you believe in and respect your self more.

Fun in life can release any tension or negativity that could be the cause to feel low-confidence.

Being grateful can be an effective way to build confidence and self-esteem, as it allows you to feel more confident within your self.

Being aware of your beliefs and implementing them will allow you to stand by your beliefs and never be a lesser person.

Be surrounded by people who are supportive people who make the most of you, making you feel more confident about yourself.

Always show kindness and appreciation to others and you'll receive the same from them. This increases your confidence.

Accept change because it is through this that anyone can progress in life and make improvements to themselves.

Make sure you take care of your needs, and ensure that you are dressed and groomed properly to ensure that others notice and admire you.

Do not at any time being a comparison with others or your life with theirs since this typically results in negative emotions and when you see people who have more advantages than you, this means that you will not feel confident around them.

Always learn from your mistakes and mistakes if you aren't looking to become stuck in one place in life or even be unable to trust yourself completely.

Set goals is another method to boost their self-confidence and self-esteem because it can provide direction, and, consequently, an end to life.

Make it a habit to give you challenges each time time. By overcoming every one you will begin believing in your capabilities and strengths and thus creating more space to build confidence.

Make sure to use affirmations regularly because they can influence the way people think and, in turn, affect the way they live their lives.

Be accountable or accountable for all of your decisions and actions. This will make you more in control of the rest of your life, and thus an enlightened person.

Always keep a record of your achievements so that you are focused and positive with the idea of the progress you're making in your life.

Be sure to never be too serious about life, and instead, take time to have enjoyment and put yourself in at ease to take in everything life can offer.

Chapter 8: Tips to Begin A Conversation

A conversation is defined as a conversation with two or more persons which is also inter-active. In essence, a conversation is two or more people conversing. It's a form of communication that takes place symmetrically and also informally, and is designed to build and sustain connections between people. Conversations are about listening and giving feedback.

Conversations are considered to be social interactions. As such they must adhere to certain rules of etiquette , and are based on the social context. The rules for communication are founded on the concept of cooperative. Failure to adhere to guidelines can result in the degrading of a conversation and, sometimes it can come at the end. The concept of cooperative communication can be classified into four conversational maxims. Four categories are employed to define the principles of rationality which are adhered to by people who follow the policy of cooperation to facilitate the effectiveness of communication.

The Maxim of Quality - It's composed of the supermaxim and submaxim. Supermaxim demands that people ensure that their contributions to a conversation genuine. Submaxims also ask individuals to refrain from expressing things they believe to be incorrect and refrain from making statements that they do not have enough evidence to back up. Quality is the key to ensuring that individuals make contributions that are more informative and meet the current need for communication. Also, individuals should refrain from providing information more than what is necessary.

Maximum of Relationship/Relevance - One must remain relevant throughout conversations. It is important to make contributions that relate to the topic and only alter when the need be.

The Maxim of Manner - The supermaxim requires one to be observant while the submaxims however will require one to steer clear of any ambiguity. To avoid the vagueness of language, one must strive to be concise, and as logical as it is.

These guidelines provide essential guidelines to ensure the effectiveness of communication. The contribution one can make during a conversation must be based on what has been stated.

Conversations that are different

If you're talking to someone it is important to be aware of the conversation that you are having. It is easy to determine this by observing the direction that the conversation you're having and also the tone. Based on tone and direction the conversations can be classified into four kinds. These include debate, dialog diatribe, discourse, and debate.

Debate - A debate can be described as a competitive and two-way exchange. The primary goal of the debate is to win the argument or convincing others. A good example of this is two students at a university who are on different sides of the political spectrum discussing the subject of politics.

Dialogue is a conversation in two ways which is collaborative. The goal of dialogue is to exchange information and establishing positive relationships among two or more persons. A good example of dialogue is two undecided university students in a conversation to try and identify the top student leaders to elect.

Discourse is a one-way and co-operative communication. The primary goal of the conversation is to convey information from a speaker or writer to listeners or readers. A typical example of a discourse conversation would be a professor giving an overview of government administration for students.

Diatribe is a single-sided communication that is highly competitive. The goal of the discussion is to express emotions, or browbeating others who don't agree with you, or to motivate people who have the same views with you. A good example is a college student discussing the results of student leader elections.

Knowing the four kinds of conversation can help you know the type of conversation that you're engaging in, and thus determine the purpose of the conversation. Knowing the reason for the conversation will allow you to talk about topics that are at the center discussion. Incorrect identification can lead to conversational mistakes, which cause it to lose the focus, and then eventually stops.

Beginning a conversation

Conversations are considered to be social interactions that assist in maintaining and building relationships. It could be a simple conversation in which people share their thoughts and ideas to people. Conversations provide chances to gain new perspectives as well as sharing your own thoughts and ideas.

In situations where you have to speak to someone who is a professional or just an acquaintance, you may not be able to consider the words and patterns of conversation. This could be different when you're talking to a family member or friend about a track you're planning to release with excitement or, in the case of someone who is not familiar with your work, they might be thinking that you're trying to persuade them to buy the track. As a skilled and experienced conversationalist you'll be able steer a conversation towards where you'd like it to go. Here are seven methods by that you can initiate the conversation and provide it with direction.

Start with a sports or weather topic could provoke a feeling of rage However, it's the most effective way to start conversation that doesn't bind you to a specific subject. Starting a conversation by discussing weather or sports offers many options for starting an opportunity to talk in a certain direction. It could be a discussion about the game you used play as a teenager or the way you're waiting for a seasonal weather change. You could start by describing how hot it is, and how the next season will let you travel on vacation and discover the beaches.

Making an idea for a Compliment to a person Compliments are among the best ways to initiate an exchange. The reason for this is because the person who receives the compliment is happy, which makes them feel warm and friendly to you and they feel free to engage in an exchange with you. When you are giving compliments, ensure that you are sincere and precise. This will ensure that you are not offending the person who received the compliment. It is important to allow the person who received the compliment to provide an opinion on the origin for the praise. In this way, you'll discover that you've gone over the topic and will give you the opportunity to think of a suitable subject. Your friend will be more open to at you and you'll enjoy a fascinating conversation.

Discussion about the venue - The location of the space you're in can serve as a great way to start conversations. For instance, if you attend an event for networking it is possible to discuss the seating arrangement or coffee. If you're in an office it is possible to discuss modifications to the room's construction. The most important thing, in this instance is to think of something that is in the space that you're in and another which your partner could also identify. If you share a similar sentiment toward the issue there is a chance that you each engage in a discussion about the character of the surroundings. If you realize that you've exhausted the subject of the environment, you could move on to come up with an alternative topic you think your partner could participate in.

Requesting a Favor Affairs - Ben Franklin came up with the idea of asking for a favour to use as a psychological trick for initiating conversations. The innate connection gets triggered when someone offers you a favor. This is due to the fact that they want to hear the things you say and how you would like to be assisted. Support does not need to be a massive issue, but it could be like asking where the restrooms are situated. After the person has helped you, you are able to quickly begin a conversation about an interesting issue.

Start with a Joke Everyone enjoys jokes. If you're looking to start conversations with others, you can make a calm and thoughtful joke that can make the person you are talking to smile, thus creating a connection. The bond you create between you two is sustained throughout the conversation. It is crucial that prior to making the joke you take into consideration the type of conversation you'd like to have in order you can make an appropriate joke. So, you'll be able to steer the conversation you're engaging in the way you want to go. A joke can also make the person you are talking to feel free to chat with you.

Beginning with an inoffensive observation The observation you make can be used to begin conversations. However, it is important to think about finding what leads to your preferred topic of conversation. You can accomplish this by pointing to something , and then asking your partner to tell you what they enjoy about it. In this way, a sequence of conversation will be created and you'll be able to steer it towards the desired goal of conversation.

A question that appears to be related to the topic you are trying to cover If people are asked particular questions they are likely to engage more deeply in the conversation they are meant to be part of. It is best to avoid asking questions that aren't directly related to your subject matter since it can cause it to seem like you're losing focus. If you ask a question about the subject you're about to discuss, will permit your partner in conversation to talk about the topic freely. One example is when you inform your friend about the music you're about to release, you could ask them if they've been listening to any good music recently. This can be an opportunity to steer the conversation toward the music you have. In this scenario you should remain glued to the conversation by asking questions and observing responses until you reach the point at which you are able to discuss your desired subject. Don't force a subject on someone because it can cause them to become disinterested. It is equally important to pose open-ended questions to let your partner to think of a range of possible answers. The answers you provide can be a good way to bring discussion on a different topic.

Tips and Tricks on Small Talk

There are a variety of situations where you're invited to occasions like a community outing or a colleague's wedding the company's event, and you are likely to meet a lot of new people. You might find yourself becoming stressed instead of happy when you realize that these situations require a little conversation. Small talk doesn't always need to be boring or involve a lot of nonsense. There are a variety of ways you can make the conversation lively and interesting.

Making Your Mind Right It is possible to spend all of your day thinking about and worrying that you'll be uneasy when you are in a social context. In this way, you'll be in a state of mind that you won't be successful when it comes to small talk. Therefore, you should create a positive mental image to go to an event, and that you will be able to meet other people with like interests as well as interact with your coworkers. In this way, you'll be able to enjoy the celebration and take part with any conversation that is brought up.

Choose who you would like to meet prior to your go to the event. It is important to think of people you'll interact with as well as those who might be sharing something that you have shared with them. You might imagine a fellow football player or someone attended the cinema with. This can aid you in coming up with ideas for the conversations you could be able to engage in.

Making a game out of it - Trying to trick your brain will make the conversation as more relaxing and enjoyable. Always try to push yourself to learn new things. It is possible to decide that you will be interacting with minimum three persons the course of a day. With these mind shifts you can reduce stress and make the conversations more enjoyable.

Always be prepared to assume the initiative to meet other people If you wish to be confident enough to talk to small groups and small conversations, don't wait long for others to come to you. Always be the first to greet person who is not yours. People's expectations that other people be the first to greet be very disappointing. So, think about taking responsibility.

Avoid being always the sidekick Being able to participate in small conversations will require you in a new way to make friends by yourself. Don't always assume to get to know someone by referring to someone you already have a relationship with.

Always be interested by listening more than you Talk - The most effective tool for making small-talk is to ask questions. Always make sure to ask open-ended questions and pay attention to the answers your partner offers to determine an appropriate topic for on your conversation. In the course of asking questions you'll discover that you are able to add some an element of substance to your conversation which makes it a more genuine conversation.

Be You - Fake networks could turn people off. To be active, it is essential to remain true to who you are and not pretend to be any aspect of your life. Always strive to be your true self.

As an introducer, when you are having a conversation there is a chance that you will encounter a guest who seems to be quite uncomfortable. One of the best things you can accomplish is inviting them into discuss the topic. This will make the discussion more interesting and lively.

Get informed about current events Be aware of current news and events will give you ideas for small-scale talks. People are always eager to listen to you because they perceive you to be knowledgeable. A well-informed opinion is something you must think about. It is also crucial to pick a subject you are interested in and that you are well-versed in.

How to keep a conversation in the right direction

One of the issues you will face at social events in which you meet new people is the obstinate silence. These situations can make you uncomfortable, and you do to stay clear of social situations. Inability to understand the best strategies to keep the conversation flowing could have a negative impact on how you interact with others. However, once you know the techniques and tricks of making sure that words flow during a conversation, you'll be able to learn a lot about the people you love and create important potential for healthy relationships and social activities.

The Reasons You're Running Out of topics to discuss in a conversation

Certain patterns of behavior can hinder your ability to have great conversations with the people whom you meet. Filtering is among the patterns. It is the reason that you always refrain from speaking about something unless you are able to determine if it's interesting, fascinating intriguing, intriguing or interesting. The other issue is difficulty in engaging in conversation. In this situation you have a difficult time to get yourself going and then engage with others who are around you. This can cause you to be surrounded by people for the entire day however, you can't engage in or participate in conversations with them.

But, acquiring new skills and techniques can help you get past the people who make it difficult to maintain the flow of words in conversations, and make you an amazing conversationalist.

Do not filter - You must attempt to express whatever is happening inside your head. Don't always check your own thoughts to determine if something is smart or interesting. You can test this technique by doing it on people whom you know well. It is best to avoid saying things that could result in you being in prison. You will realize that speaking out does not mean that people will look at your character. Most of the time, people will be focused on the message they intend to communicate the words you use and not on the quality of what you are saying.

Engaging in conversation using phrases that motivate your partner to continue speaking This strategy is effective to keep a conversation moving. A few of the phrases that you can employ include "interesting and interesting, tell me about it", "wow how you have handled it." If you can show your audience that you're keen on the conversation and they keep talking and will enjoy speaking to you. The phrases you employ during the conversation show your friend that you are curious about what they are saying and it gives them a reason to keep on talking with you.

Finding stories from Everywhere It is a crucial method to ensure that a conversation keeps in a continuous flow. When stories are included in the discussion, it gets more intriguing. It is not enough to talk about your life experiences, but attempt to create stories from every aspect of life. For instance, you could relate the experiences of people who you have met or people you've seen in TV, magazines or on the radio. The ability to incorporate stories into your conversations is simple when you know how to make use of these stories. You've experienced or frequently heard stories, and you're confident about their authenticity. When you hear someone mention something related to the incident and you want to share the story to them. This adds an additional dimension in the discussion. People will be more open to you when you freely share these experiences with them.

The most important thing to do in maintaining a conversation is applying the tips to the person you're meeting. Avoid overburdening yourself by using all of the strategies at the same time, but you should you should try each one at a different point. The knowledge gained from one technique will increase your confidence as you apply other strategies in interactions.

How to end a conversation

Although a conversation may be engaging, you might need to conclude the conversation before your partner is willing. It is therefore important to conclude the conversation in a manner and not appear at them as rude. There are numerous ways you can close the conversation, like by using words or by with body language. This is a great way to conclude the conversation. Below are some guidelines to help you conclude the conversation with grace.

Closing with a positive note Wrapping up the conversation with using positive words can allow you to conclude the conversation in a positive manner. You can accomplish this by thanking your conversation partner for their time, thereby giving a signal that you're ready to end the conversation. Sometimes, conversations can seem to last for a long time and you'll need to wait for your partner to finish what they're talking about. It is possible to look them in the eye and say things such as, "I'm so humbled that you took the time to allow us to speak" or "thank you for taking the time." If you are in a situation when your spouse doesn't realize what you are saying to stop talking, you can use phrases like, "well, thank you again and I'm really ready to move on."

The waiting for a lull in a Conversations to end A conversation, no matter its content, it will always have an unnatural gap. If you are looking to end the conversation, you may take a few moments of silence, and then inform your companions that you are thinking, "wow, it has been a pleasure talking with you, but I need to start talking."

Making future Plans Presenting specific plans is a great and courteous method to end the conversation. It can show your companion the fact that you've had a wonderful conversation with them and you'd like to have a longer conversation with them. It is important to wait until the speaker has finished the conversation and then ask questions like, "what are you up to this weekend/ Do you wish to have a glass of wines?" You can also share your contact details with the person you are talking to, and discuss exchanging emails or messages to discuss plans.

Conversations can seem simple to start, carry on and then end with a bang However, it is important to master some methods to have a successful conversation. Everyone should try to keep the conversation as lively as they can, thereby fostering friendships and experiencing new things.

Chapter 9: Innovative Methods to Start Small Talks

If you've figured out the potential topics you can discuss, it's the time to determine how to get it done and start the discussion. Be aware that, even the best you know about potential topics for small talk topics however, you'll still be unable to pull it off if aren't certain how to present it. This chapter will provide several of the important strategies that will help you through this stage.

Ask open-ended questions.

Many people like to speak about themselves, and engaging in this type of conversation is an excellent way to start small conversations and keep the conversation running. Questions that are open to discussion require explanations rather than a simple either or. They usually begin with the words is, who, what they are framed with where, how, why, and when. Closed questions however start with the words are/am/is have and have. One example of an open-ended question is: What kind that music you like most and what is it? It's not uncommon for open questions to require an explanation and you're able to get just a simple"yes or no" as an answer. Because there's a reason it is possible to reply and prolong the conversation.

Recall earlier discussions

If you're going to be speaking with someone who you've spoken to previously, it is ideal to keep your own list of subjects you've discussed before. Then, you can continue to talk about the same topic. One example would be an unpleasant news story he relayed to you, an idea that he's working on or a recent accomplishment of your child. In addition to giving you an idea of what you can discuss as well, it may help the other person feel betteras it indicates that you're paying the message he's expressing. It lets him know how great of a listener and also that you are interested in the problems and experiences the other person shared with you. It can also encourage him to create a bond.

Ask him questions that he will quickly answer

For you to be able to effectively start small discussions to ensure that the conversation keeps moving, be sure to make sure which the other party will have no trouble in answering or responding to. Remember that there are certain types of questions that are difficult to respond to. If you are looking to make someone feel comfortable, ask simple and intriguing questions that he'll want to know the answer to. This will to ensure that conversations be more enjoyable and flow more easily which will make both of you more relaxed.

Be mindful

It's not a good idea to be adamant about asking someone questions without considering whether they're willing to discuss the subject that you're looking for. When you ask him questions ensure that it's not invasive. It shouldn't be related to issues they don't wish to talk about. For example some people might feel angry or upset when you inquire about things that impact their personal lives. This includes weight, insufficient qualifications or abilities, relationships problems, etc. Be mindful and sensitive. Avoid discussing matters that might interfere with the privacy of your loved ones or cause them to feel guilty about their own self-esteem.

Name the person you're talking with at times

Apart from aiding you in remembering his name, it's an excellent method of showing respect for him and make him feel at ease. Making reference to him by his name will help make the conversation more intimate, personal and genuine. This can create more connections and trust, so don't be shocked when you realize that the conversation you had started has turned into a much smarter, more profound and significant one.

Stay engaged

You must ensure that you don't appear bored while you are talking to anyone. You want him to feel that you're truly engaged in the conversation you've initiated and are interested in what he's talking about.

Let him know how committed to keep the conversation going. Concentrate on him as equally. Keep your attention at a high level, and not trying to regress from yourself. This is a crucial step in order to maintain the conversation in a relaxed and pleasant conversation. Ensure that the conversation continues.

The benefit of engaging yourself for the entire time you talk to the person you are talking to is that it will provide you with ideas for things to discuss during your subsequent small talk and conversations. This is particularly important in the event that you're likely to speak with the same person over and over. This can instantly provide you with some idea of what you might be able to talk regarding, for instance, seeking an update on some aspect of his life.

Be yourself

When you are starting small discussions it's not necessary to pretend to be like someone you're not , as this will only cause you to feel uncomfortable. Do what you are comfortable with. React to situations according to the way you usually respond. Smile and laugh naturally every when someone comes up with a joke or humorous remarks. Do not force laughter you might be alarming him. Smile and smile naturally. Just be yourself and you'll most likely express these actions naturally, instead of making them appear awkward and forced.

Do not worry about the pauses

It's not a problem in the event that there's a pause following the discussion of an issue. The great thing about the pauses is that you could effectively use them to switch the topic. They also function as an opportunity to take a brief break or a breather, and then re-energize small talk. There's no need to be concerned unless the silence or pause is getting too lengthy. Do not stress yourself so long as you allow yourself for a bit or simply move on to the next topic, you're good to go.

Don't be afraid to go a bit more intimate

This is an excellent idea, provided that you decide first whether the other person is open to discussing things that are personal to them. The benefit of becoming more intimate and with the permission of the other party, is that you have an opportunity to connect to him quicker. It is easy to become acquainted with him, which makes it simpler to establish connections. A few safe topics that aren't too personal, you can chat with him about could be his favourite book, his most favored team, his interests and interests, as well as his most loved holiday.

Ask follow-up questions

After you've started the conversation, be certain to be attentive to his replies. This can be a big help in weaving in good follow-up questions. Follow-up questions can keep the conversation running. Be sure to do not over-interrogate to avoid causing him irritation. The questions you ask him should be answered by something that he is comfortable with.

Do not make your small talk your partner uncomfortable, too. Be aware of his reactions whether they are either verbally or not. It is also recommended to be more polite in your responses to those who are uneasy or uncomfortable with. When the individual you're speaking to isn't interested in sharing details or details or is uninterested, avoid talking to them for too long.

When asking follow-up questions are crucial to keep the conversation running, it is important to know when to end the conversation. Beware of asking too many questions when he begins to lose interest.

Chapter 10: Tips to Manage a tense conversation

Everybody has at least one time in their life when they were involved in a tense small-talking situation. Sometimes, they could have made a few faux pas in conversations "sins". Whatever the case you should be aware of how to avoid these mistakes in the future , so that you are in the process of becoming an improved conversationalist.

The Pregnant Pause

Your conversation partners are chatting with each other for a good twenty minutes about an issue. Everyone is laughing and wiping the tears from your eyes and then suddenly everyone is silent and isn't sure what to say. If this ever occurs, all you need to do is introduce an opportunity to start a conversation. Here are some suggestions to help you think about the possibilities:

Have you seen the latest film starring ...?

By the way, could anyone recommend me an excellent financial advisor, hairdresser or French teacher?

Have seen the newest gadget known as ...? I just finished reading this book, titled .... Did you had a chance to read it?

With a jump-starter you are able to either remain on the same subject that you and your friends are currently discussing, or ask a new question regarding something you've been interested in recently. Now you're viewed as the hero who brought everyone back from the uncomfortable silence.

The Nosy Conversationalist

There's a fine line between someone engaging in conversation and one who asks so numerous questions that they sound like someone from an FBI agent. Someone who ends up appearing more snarky than genuine is the one who asks an endless amount of questions, leaving one person very little space to reply. This is when the person who is talking becomes an inmate. He or she is no longer elaborate or even ask questions themselves.

If you're guilty employing this approach to interrogation the best thing you can do is stop yourself from getting caught when you are in the middle of asking too many questions, and let the person finish their answers first. If you're an endless questioning of a companion, then you should try to control your conversation and ask questions too like asking them what their job is for money. After that, you can gradually ease into a more relaxed rhythm by asking questions in the follow-up and letting them inquire again every now and then.

The Line-shooter

Braggarts is a hassle for listeners, particularly when they pair the braggart with making people feel inferior to him. Every conversation you have goes back to the way he or achieved a particular accomplishment, and there's plenty of information on the subject. If you find yourself in an exchange with a line shooter the best thing you can do is bring your conversation to something which is far more broad.

If, for instance, that person is constantly talking about the cost of a vacation that she's been on You can then discuss the current events in that area, for example, when you say, "speaking of Italy, have you seen on the news lately about the recent events in Italy?" ..." Italy-related scandal?" There's no need to fight those who are uninhibited and the best thing one can accomplish is move the conversation in a different direction with ease.

The Monopolist

The monopolist loves the spotlight. The person who controls the conversation and desires to be heard and is unable to listen to other people. A person who is a conversation monopolist believes that he is doing everyone the favor of maintaining the momentum. What was supposed to be an exchange turns into an uni-man-oratory.

To ensure that you don't become a monopolist, make sure you do not talk for longer than 5 minutes. You should always remember to seek out your friend's opinion, take note of what they have to speak. If you're talking to a monopolist You have a myriad of options, among which is to exercise the art of active listening with him. This is essential for monopolizers who are your boss, client or family member you wish to impress.

If you're trying to disarm the monopolist and let other people or you talk for a while you can make an interception. Be on the lookout for an interval then reply with"something like "That's is a great idea Marie. How are you doing, Agatha How's your office?"

There are a lot other awkward conversations out in the world than these four scenarios. It's your decision to figure out how to guide the conversation from uncomfortable to friendly. So long as you maintain a polite, sincere and pleasant manner you will be able to overcome every small conversation obstacle on the path.

Chapter 11: Everything to Do with Being Present

As well as finding an agreement with someone by using the various strategies which were discussed earlier in this chapter one of the most important things you need to be aware of when you want to master informal conversations is the concept of being present.If the person you're speaking feels that you're not listening , or that you're distracted by other things going on It's likely that the person will begin be irritated and eventually interact with you in unsatisfactory way.This section will examine the concept of being present in the modern world of technology and what you can do to ensure that you are being present in a small chat, even though you're feeling boring.

Technology's grip on our attention

Nowadays, it may be more difficult than ever to be present in our lives.Our smartphones have evolved into an entertainment center that is constantly connected to our fingers, which means that it it harder than ever to interact with people around us in positive and respectful ways.We've experienced an environment where it's simpler to behave as if something you do on your phone is significant, instead of taking the time to go out and look for people to converse to.This book will assist you in resisting this urge, no matter if you have your phone within your possession.Some useful tips you can use when faced by this kind of scenario is to place your phone in a location that can't be easily reached for example, within your car.Another useful idea is to set your phone in silent mode when you know that you'll be in a situation that may require a brief conversation for more time.Our smartphones are addictive and these strategies could take some time getting used to, but this doesn't make them less valuable.

Looping and Dipping

Small conversations can be boring for anyone of us (yes this includes myself).Sometimes subjects in small talk can be boring. That's why you need different strategies to increase our enjoyment of small talk, and be engaging regardless of our minds restraining against it.When you notice your mind is wandering far away from those you're talkingto, you may use a method that's called looping or dipping.All you need to do to be successful with this technique is attempt to repeat back to the person to whom you're communicating the information that they're telling you.This is a great technique, particularly for those whose brain tends to wander away from a conversation. conversation.Often we tend to talk about what we think of the situation, instead of really listen to what it is that the person on the other end of the conversation saying.When you can stay on top of the details of a conversation, and also gain the perspective of someone else and gain their perspective, you'll have greater satisfaction staying in the present and attentive.

Responding by Tact

After you've completed the looping technique and dips and the person on the opposite end of the discussion is confirming that you do actually understand their point of view clearly, you must try to address their arguments using your own thoughts instead of responding on their comments.This is crucial due to two reasons.The second reason is when you are able to formulate your own thoughts about a topic, rather than simply reacting to another's view regarding the subject and dipping, you'll notice that the conversation is more engaging than it normally would be since you have formulated an entirely new perspective or method of thinking about the topic to hand.The third reason when you express your opinion in response to another's opinion, there's an opportunity to appear more hostile than you intend particularly if you hold opinions that are completely different from that person's.Remember that small talk is about making the conversation as casual as possible. The less controversial you are able to be the more comfortable.

Writing down your thoughts

In the event that you're one who regularly has an abundance of thoughts bouncing around in your mind at any given moment, it's beneficial to periodically note down any random thoughts you're having. When you do this, you're taking your thoughts into your own space and will enable you to be more attentive when speaking to people and trying to start an interesting conversation. There's no harm in having a scattered brain in the long run, provided you're able to shut off the other portion of your mind at least once every time.

Being present is important when you're trying to maintain any type of conversation, but it can be argued that it is especially important during small talk. Admittedly, small talk is often not about the most interesting topics on the planet, but this is why being present is so important. Additionally, you have to remember that if this is the first time that you're talking to someone, then you are going to be making a first impression on this person.Do you want to come off as someone who is seems to be aloof and caught up in your own head?Or do you want to come off as someone who is a good conversationalist, is positive, and could potentially be a good friend to have later on down the line?The choice is entirely yours, and your actions often dictate how you will be portrayed.The simple fact of the matter is that if you want to be perceived negatively, constantly being on your phone or pretending that you're listening when you're actually not is the perfect way to achieve this.

Chapter 12: Building a Career And Business Using Small Talk

People who excel in small talk are experts in making people feel valued and at ease. That goes far to bolster to a business relationship and concluding a deal, or leading to a career. The best part about communicating abilities is that anyone can master these skills. The majority of those who are successful in their chosen field are experts in communicating. They achieved their goals as a professional or even in the context of the business they run.

Career

Is small talk essential in establishing your career? Do you think small talk can aid the growth in your professional career? Research on small talk shows that it isn't going to make an unexperienced job seeker however, the more experienced job seeker is more likely to find a job after some well-planned and tactical strategically placed small talks.

As per research from the Kellogg Business School, the recent hiring results did not based on skills or experience alone. were the sole basis for assessment. The results of employment depend on the individual's lifestyle, and that was more important than skills and experience in evaluating the result. One of the easiest ways to talk to and assess your hobbies, interests, and cultural preferences is through the utilization of conversation from the start up to the final interview. So, using small talk can help you in securing an interview and can have an enormous positive impact in the field you choose to pursue.

Additionally, it is a place that focuses on tactical conversation helps you locate the openings in employment and jobs through referral. Additionally, it helps to build trust and increase the likelihood of networks offering you a job open. We all know the fact that hiring referrals is a common method of job seekers employed. According to a study the most popular method to get an employment opportunity is via the referral method, with one in four chance of securing an employment. If you've got the ability and proficiency to make small talk effectively, so why not make use of it at the context of an event like gatherings, parties and conferences to create contacts that can help you land the job you want through the referral.

These networks that you have created through small talk do not only increase the likelihood of finding jobs and also increase your chances of getting the job. According to research, that referred applicants have two times more likely to be invited to an interview than applicants who are not referred, and also have a higher percentage of being offered the job.

It is clear about the benefit of small talk helping job seekers advance their careers through the creation of strong personal networks that aid in getting them referred to and subsequently selected for positions. Naturally, not just the ability to talking will get you an employment. It is still necessary to have enthusiastic, competent and competent however, networking through using small talk is an essential element to get the job you want and furthering your career.

Business

Small Talk is beneficial for business. It's not a an untruth that building strong relationships with your customers is a great idea for business. Alongside learning the art of conversation, and a high-quality products or services can be the key to success. It is crucial to ensure that each employee at your company is proficient with the craft of small-talk. The employees should engage each client with a conversation that makes the client feel at ease before they even receive the service that your company offers.

In business meetings it is a chance for people to build each other's reputation and level of knowledge. If there's already a bond between two people, the short conversation serves as an beginning before moving on to more substantive discussions. It permits them to express their personal style and feel the mood of the other.

In the workplace small talk tends to happen mostly between colleagues with the same skills. However, it could be employed by the boss to build connections with their employees under their supervision. An employer who demands their employees to work extra hours could attempt to motivate them with small talk in order to temporarily reduce the gap in terms of position. The degree of stability between a conversations and small talk in the workplace is dependent on the circumstances and is also affected by the authority of the two people speaking. It is usually the person with higher status is the one who decides the conversation, since they are the ones who have the authority to conclude the conversation.

Another method to improve relationships between employees at the area is to make use of names. Make use of the name of the person to begin the conversation. This helps you remember the name of the person and inform the person that you're speaking to them in particular. This increases the chances of engaging in conversation with people and makes them more curious the topic, particularly how you even know his name. Do not lie by using a different names to address them, some people not like it. It's better to inquire about the name of someone in case you've forgotten his or the name of the person.

The most effective way to establish solid relationships with your customer is. When you earn the trust of your client and they consider you a friend, regardless of the amount of competition or great deals they get from your competitors. They'll still be tempted to buy or use your services.

The cheapest and most effective in marketing your business is to engage in small conversations. Small talk is essential for building and enhancing business relationships. Always begin and conclude your business conversations with a conversation to enhance your relationship. Financial planners are sought-after by investors because of their ability to help them feel safe and secure as they can for their financial security.

Chapter 13: Small Talk Starters

Since this book is focused on small talk, I'll review some common small talk prompts. The small talk openers can be described as the icebreakers can be used to begin conversations in any setting.

Small talk is usually shared in small groups of people, or even two people in a variety of circumstances. If you're in circumstances, such as taking a train ride and you are reading the newspaper you notice that your fellow traveler are also reading that same paper and you begin to engage in conversation.

Whatever you decide to begin with, the majority of small talk starters share three characteristics.

They're not intruding: Small conversations are not meant to invade one's privacy. They are intended to be casual conversation between friends. Therefore, before you even begin with a conversation that is small it is important to make sure that the conversations are not overly intruding.

They're authentic: Make sure your talk starters are authentic. If you steer the small-talk in a way that you're uncomfortable with, you will lose the story, and also the desire to continue the small conversation. Therefore, it is crucial that your openings sound as authentic as the topics you discuss.

They're adapted to for: You shouldn't begin a conversation about the rainy weather when it is summer. You'll be a fool. You adjust your introduction to the specific situation. In the case that you're on an train carriage, the starting point could be "Hello. I'm sure you're reading the same paper that you were reading. Did you discover anything interesting in the news of today?"

A few interesting ideas are listed below for your convenience.

In addition to the standard Hello, Hi, Good Morning Good Evening as well as the usual Hello, Good Morning, Good Evening, Good Morning, and so on. You can also begin conversations using the phrases that follow.

What are your thoughts about this event, party or gathering? A simple and easy question to ask at an event or or gathering

Do you know anyone here? When you run into somebody you've known in a brand new area

What are you working in? - excellent starter at networking events

Have you been there before? When you go to the first time and are looking to start the conversation

WOW... this is an incredible watch! Where did you buy it? If you love the look of a watch worn by someone else.

Why not begin with a story about yourself? This is a common way to start in interviews.

Have you seen the latest scandals that have occurred in the world of soccer? When you realize that someone else is equally fascinated by soccer's world.

Where do you come from? If you meet someone from a different nation

I've had a very long and tiring day. What about you? When you get together with an acquaintance after a long day at work

What drink will you be having? At a dinner get together with your buddies

These are a few common ideas that can be used in a variety of situations.

These aren't only the "only" starters can be used. Based on the circumstances it is possible to make use of a range of starters to aid in keeping a conversation going with your friends.

While you are reading this book, I'll provide some real and hypothetical instances that you can identify with and know how to start small talk, and then continue them.

If you are engaging in conversation with others it is important to be sure to adhere to certain manners of speech.

Be attentive, and don't be involved in any dispute

Keep eye contact with people you talk to

Don't be afraid to express your opinion, no matter how silly it might sound.

Never be critical of others.

Be open to other's points of view.

Begin small talk in a polite manner

Know when to stop the conversation

These are the most important points that I think you must be aware of. There are many more information from different websites, however I think that this is enough.

Before closing this chapter, I'll provide you with a few other small talk ideas.

What's the most exciting thing you've ever done?

What's the meaning behind your name?

Do you remember the most happy moment in your life?

What is the most painful moment of your life?

Tell me something about you.

If you had to look back on the past, whom would you wish to have the opportunity to talk to and why?

Which athlete is your top choice and why?

What is the furthest location you've been away from home?

Which was the most recent country you've traveled to?

Where do you want to be in 10 years' time?

Write about the latest book you've read?

What is your your favorite book?

Do you want to describe your most trusted friend from school?

What is your favorite friend from college?

What is your favorite friend? What do you enjoy about them?

Write about your high school experience in a few paragraphs.

Tell us about your first memory.

What is your definition of God?

If you had the chance to go back in your past and change something that you would wish to change about your history?

What is your most cherished Bible verse?

Which Biblical person do you identify with the most?

Which is your most favored Disney character?

What is your favorite cartoon person?

What is the definition of religion?

Do you think that you are a Christian?

Which gadget would you want to own?

Which is your most-loved holiday destination?

What would be the most important thing you'd like your parents to say to you today?

What is your most-loved drink?

What is your most favorite fruit?

What is your most-loved dish?

What happens when you start to feel discouraged?

If God granted you a blessing then what would you ask for?

If you came across Aladdin's magic lamp What could you decide to do?

If you had supernatural powers, what would be the first thing you'd like to alter in the world?

If you were asked to serve as the president of the USA for a single day What would you accomplish during the course of the day?

What new skills do you need to develop over the next 6 months or a year?

The most influential person you know? And why?

Do you think that music could aid in developing your character?

What is your top artist?

What is your mantra in your life?

What is your most fav outfit or dress?

Do you have a glimpse of God in your everyday life?

If you had the most extensive collection of something What would that thing be?

What is the thing that you're most regretful about in your life?

Have you had a nickname from your childhood? What's the story of the name?

Which is your most fav movie actor?

What is your most fav movie?

How would you react if wild lion appeared before you?

What's your purpose in your life?

If you were able to bring back a deceased person to their former life whom would it be?

What is your typical day at college?

Are you a pet owner at your home?

What is your most-loved or most-loved day?

What's the last thing you do prior to getting ready for bed?

If you had the chance to meet any historical figure whom would you choose?

What is your favourite hobby?
Do you study music? Or play an instrument that is musical?
What kind of child was you?
Define your dream job.
What are (was) your top topic?
Have you ever been in trouble in school?
Do you believe that love is from the first moment?
Do you believe you're an Alpha male?
If you had $1billion, would you still go to classes or working?
What was your favorite teacher at school, college or university?
Which of your features do you love the most?
Is there something that is first that you find appealing about a male or girl?
What was your most unpleasant vacation memory?
Which is your top flavor of ice cream?
What is your favorite dish?
Tell us about the latest movie you've watched?
What do you find most frightening?

What's the best piece of advice you've received?

What's the most bizarre thing you've done up to now?

What is the most deceitful lie you've ever told?

Do you ever lie? Why and when?

Do you have faith or practice other religious beliefs?

What other religion, aside that your own do prefer?

Do you prefer coffee or tea?

What is your first vehicle? Tell us about it.

Do you believe that you are naturally good?

If you were stuck on an island with your ideal guy or person, which one would it be?

Which season is your absolute favorite?

Which is your preferred place to live? Rural or in urban areas?

The most gorgeous city that you have ever been to?

Do you sing when bathing? In other words, are you singing in the bathroom?

If you were the King of a country what country would it be?

What's your ideal your ideal date?

What are the qualities you would like your partner to possess?

What was that first moment you shared with someone?

Have you learned another language?

Have you ever handed an infringement ticket because of speeding?

Which one is your most loved car?

Who are you closest to the most - your father or mother?

What was the most difficult thing you've had to do?

If today was your last day on earth How would you spend it?

If you only had 30 minutes left to live, what would you say to your spouse?

What are three traits you admire from your parents?

Define the first time you worked for your job.

Which is your preferred place to live? In a city or in the country?

What is your most-loved food item during the week?

What is your most loved animal?

Where are wild animals most easily observed - in the zoo as well as in wild?

Did you go on the African Safari?

What is your favourite flower?

What is your most favorite fruit?

What is the most personal experience you've faced?

What is your biggest weakness?

What is your strongest strength?

If you had the chance to be as an animal, what kind of animal would you want to be?

If you had the opportunity to have an hour free time each day what would you do with your time?

Write about a trait you admired from your mother the most.

Write about a quality you admired with your father the most.

What characteristics do your siblings share that you admire the most?

How many siblings do you have?

Who was your first famous crush?

If you were on an island and were accompanied by someone famous Who would that celebrity be?

What is the most difficult thing for you to accomplish?

What is your most-loved dessert?

What is your top phone brand?

What are the qualities you admire in Steve Jobs?

What was your most loved childhood toy?

When you are reading in the following chapter keep in mind that small talks are intended to be of a short duration they are not meant to last for long durations. The average duration of small talks ranges from 20 minutes to a half hour. Rarely the duration can exceed 45 minutes.

Chapter 14: Small Talk Starter Guide

Being being an introvert I'm probably not the most vocal in most situations.I'm more comfortable 1 on 1 however in group settings it's sometimes difficult to join in or to want to do so really.This section is devoted to guidelines and even a few lines for getting small conversations going.
Questions to start a conversation
What was the first job you've ever held?
This question is asked by people from a variety of cultures.Almost all people have to work to live.It might even trigger laughter at the beginning due to the absurd actions we engage in as children.
What is your ideal superpower?
This is a bit ridiculous and maybe not appropriate for younger people or for

someone older who appears to be a little more trendy and not grouchy.I prefer to respond by saying "Double Jump" because everyone is interested in invisibility and immortality, as well as flying the basics.Silly questions deserve a humorous answer, I'd say.

What are the foods you would not take in? This is a good twist on asking "what's your favourite food" and can make the other person change their thoughts to think a bit.This could start off as an "o nice question you'll have to think about it" type of conversation starter.So you might want to prepare your answer for the event that the person you are talking to is caught off guard.I recommend avoiding asking the "what is your favourite song" as well as "what is your most favorite color" absurd cliches.

Did you recently read any of your favorite books? or listen to of the best podcasts?

We've cast more of a net as certain people don't really know how to read, so it offers them an alternative of the "not at all, not really" answer that could sabotage the conversation.

Conversational Pathways

Request Advice

This could make someone else feel, based on the topic very comfortable since you're placing a lot of trust in their opinion.People like to discuss their views, so this can ignite the perfect conversation.

Avoid Your Favorite Topics

The issue is that you could speak too much due to your level of interest in the subject.If you don't exhibit the same level of enthusiasm, they may not even touch the topic but go on, unless they're truly in the area.

Do Not Use Your Phone

This can be extremely annoying for nearly anyone.People who are constantly looking at their phone or send texts when you're talking to them is quite distracting.I adhere to a common policy that I will not check my mobile when someone else is not around or if I receive an incoming phone call.I usually respond with the traditional "so Sorry, but have to do this" in response to the call display.Depending on the significance of the call, the rule can be a bit adaptable, but do not ignore someone else because of a phone call that isn't nice.

Traffic Light Rule

Mark Goulston at the Harvard Business Review discusses a technique employed by radio hosts that is known as"Traffic Light Rule "Traffic Light Rule".The concept is that in the initial 20 seconds during which you speak all is well, and the person you are talking to likes the person as long as the assertion is meaningful and serves the other person.Unless you're very skilled at speaking, people who are talking for more than an hour at a time are boring and viewed as too chatty.The subsequent 20 seconds are an orange light as the possibility of losing person's attention heightens.At the point of 40 seconds your light will turn red.Obviously it is possible to make exceptions for all things and extending your the time that someone is interested could be acceptable, however this can be a great little test.

Small talk can have a variety of advantages for your psyche.I am aware that a conversation that is awkward could make you feel depressed too or make you feel weird.The same way a positive conversation can get you excited and eager to go.This is the excitement of small talk. We aren't sure where it will take us, but because we do not know the person, the potential to be random is there.There is no danger of small talk, and unlimited upside.What are you at risk of offending someone else? The most likely way for someone to hurt your feelings is if you say something that was offensive and got around so that people would disapprove of you.The aspect to consider is, you can also make a statement that is offending to a friend, too with the same outcome.The benefit of not being able to familiar with the other person gives the possibility to dismiss things as jokes, however in general, do not engage in conversations which could be offensive to someone.That's part of our fundamental rules section, and it is applies to all conversations. applies.A study from University of Michigan. University of Michigan shows that people with soft skills tend to get a higher-paying job in addition to being productive.Small talks, or communication skills are a significant aspect of the soft skills.If you can improve your small talk and getting better in your communication, you will increase your productivity and earn more money, then why aren't we doing it more often?

A common belief across nearly all fields has been that "connections matter".Well If this is true, then why not create those connections? all have our own biases on the way we view individuals, but you don't be aware of how connected your life or the one you would like to be part of might be.Some of the most flashiest dressed and most expensive cars driving people are totally broke.That man in sweatpants with an old shirt with a tiny stain could have five houses across the world.We don't have a clue who we'll encounter or have an exchange with, but if we get the chance, why not grab it.The issue with having a job, interviewing as well as working with clients and colleagues is that conversation is an essential requirement.There is a trend to remote work in the present and more and more non-social jobs are appearing across all over the place, however as a general majority, jobs require dealing with people.Sometimes things that aren't crucial to you is essential to a person who is a client customer.This is the reason small talk can be helpful to you, particularly if you're proficient in it. are able to make introductions, and then play games such as looking for new ideas or details based on your experiences studying body movements and like.

Small talk is regarded as an act of respect to many people.If you attend an event and you talk to everyone , but leave the person who you haven't met before what do you think they'll feel? Involve them in the conversation , or talk to them a bit to ensure they feel comfortable.It's always pleasant to see someone come up and be genuine with you, instead of just "announce that they're there" nearly.

Tips for Introverts

There are some things that introverts can try in order to be more comfortable engaging in small conversations.

The first thing to do is attempt to reduce your anxiety.I recently began meditating for a short time throughout the day. It has certainly helped in relaxing even for just a bit.Things such as caffeine, which is an stimulant, could make you more anxious, and even if you believe you require the boost. However, there is a some trade offs.Staying positive and making things easy and pleasant is the best way to reduce anxiety.When things get serious , the silences can seem more severe.

Remaining with the belief that a conversation is useless or that it is going to be boring can ruin any conversation from the start.Going into the conversation with more positive energy and trying to connect with the other person , or discover something new from their experience that could even benefit you.Who is sure but we know that if we aren't able to get your conversation moving, there is no way to make it happen.This could also be a good way to tie into paying attention.You could get lost in your thoughts about what the next thing you'll do instead of listening.Listening involves asking questions about topics you're really interested in is easier.You will not be tempted to ask irrelevant questions that they might have already answered when you lost in your own mind.

The ability to discern signals from someone else is key.If they are finishing an entire sentence and begin to make a move toward the exit or perhaps moving a little after every tiny conversation, they will want to leave.I've been stopped a couple of occasions by individuals who appear to carry on and on.Although an engaging conversation could be enjoyable, it can also lead to learning new things, or perhaps becoming a friend it is important to be attentive to cues.If you see someone else near to saying something or if they are rushing into conversation, perhaps you can put your thoughts aside and inquire as to what they are planning to say.This is contingent upon their response to what you have said If they don't nod when you've said something but try to jump into the conversation, it might be done.Also make sure you don't go on in the middle of a conversation after someone tries to get involved in the conversation, because most times, people forget what they had in mind to say as they try to listen to what.

Chapter 15: Ending Conversation

There are two scenarios in which you have to conclude the conversation.The one is when you must finish it because you have to and the second one is due to the reason you wanted to. In both instances it can be a difficult task.

How to end the conversation In a respectful manner

A sudden departure from the group could be considered impolite.However by following these tried and true techniques below, you can close your conversation with a polite manner.

Use a vague or false excuse that is based on factual.

A vague excuse could be considered rude when it's obvious.But when it's an excuse based on something real, the other participants to the conversation might not be in a hurry to stop you.

A vague excuse for the weather or time is the most common way to end the conversation.But it is important to utilize them in a smart way.

The excuse that you need to leave due to appointments with your customer on a Sunday could be seen as a flims excuse.But the fact that you are using it on a workday could be viewed as legitimate reason.

If you tell your coworkers that you need to end the meeting early because an aunt is due to arrive to visit could be an untrue excuse.But when you inform them that you must bring your child to the morning, they will not resist your request to keep you in the loop.

The reason you don't want to talk due to the imminent rain is a legitimate excuse even if you don't possess either a car or umbrella.But even if you do are protected from rain, it might be seen as a valid reason.

Find a substitute.

If you'd like to stop the conversation but the other party evidently not interested in ending the conversation take it off, think about offering the substitute.Pull someone else into the conversation and help them feel at ease in the presence of another party.Then you can gradually decrease your involvement, and let them to speak to one other.Once they're having fun with one another, gently tap your shoulder with one and then excuse yourself and leave.

It is important to be cautious when selecting the person you host, though.Make sure that the other party has an reaction.If the guest is not a good conversationalist, you could end up being engaged for a longer period of time.

Find a different venue.

In this case in this scenario, you will direct the other party that you're going to quit the conversation, but you have invited them to a party or gathering so that you could continue the conversation.You are able to use this tactic even though you do not intend to keep the conversation going.

You could simply tell them, "I really have to go.Let's organize a gathering or get together to continue the discussion another time."The other person may not think about your invitation after your departure or even after the day has ended.

If someone else wants to know when, simply tell them that you'll call him.If you'd like to talk to him once more, make the call.If you don't, avoid calling him.He could forget about it later.

Always make sure to say goodbye in a professional manner.

Don't just disappear suddenly.Whatever the reason or method when you leave the conversation, you must always offer an appropriate goodbye."I'm deeply sorry that I need to leave," "It was a pleasure meeting you once more," "I would like to see you once more," are just a few examples of the phrases that you can utilize to say your final goodbye.

After you have said your goodbyes in a proper manner to the other party, they would allow you to leave without an issue.

Things to Avoid when ending an exchange

Don't stop your conversation by disobeying the speaker.

Sometimes, ignoring the speaker might work.He might notice your lack of interest and stop the conversation naturally.But the speaker will consider you to be unkind to him.

Be sure to not shift your attention to something else in the course of an exchange.

Certain people make use of props to end the conversation.They might change their watches or tie during the conversation.Some might read magazines while another are speaking.These are desperate ways to stop the conversation. It is possible to avoid a negative conversation, but also received a negative reputation.

Chapter 16: Effective Small Talk Begins with Confidence

It's easy to imagine that people who are socially functioning and comfortable with their role in social settings were created this way. They didn't. There is no way to be 100% free of self-doubt when socializing. There is always the chance that something or someone causes anxiety or nervousness.

But, those who appear to be at ease with other people tend to not let doubts about themselves limit their success. They take on the challenge face-to-face and put themselves in different social settings repeatedly. That's the secret to becoming socially proficient. That's the secret to ensuring your place in any social gathering. It's all about practice.

Imagine playing a game. The more you train the movements the more efficient and responsive you become in time. It is not necessary to visualize the movements at all times however your body will perform better and more efficiently. This is referred to as muscle memory. You can apply the same principle to improve your social skills.

Socially successful is the result of a lot of practice over time. It's about pushing yourself out of your home and taking the lessons and knowledge that these experiences provide. The only way to improve your social confidence is to go out and meet new people. I would like to claim that you will first be confident and then to socialize, but the reality of the matter is seeing your proficiency in the area that provides confidence in your abilities.

What is it to be Confident and How it Reduces Social Anxiety

Self-confidence is the state of confidence in your capabilities and your worth as an individual who is evident to other people. "Confidence" originates in the Latin word fidere which is a reference to "to believe in yourself." Confidence in yourself is about trusting yourself. It's about knowing that you are able to be up to the challenge and take on new challenges and be able to cope difficult situations. It is about accepting responsibility.

Self-confidence should not be confused as arrogance. Arrogance is the attitude of superiority which manifests as an arrogant attitude. Many people believe that being confident means you need to be skilled at something or be extremely successful in general. However, this isn't the case. There are many self-confident people who claim to be masters of all trades, and masters of nothing. There are many confident individuals that aren't what the majority of people would call successful.

In the end, real confidence is based on the knowledge that it's okay to not be able to answer all your questions. It is acceptable to fall short from time to time. It is knowing that you're not defined by moment or the circumstance regardless of whether they're positive or negative. It also means knowing that you're not measured by any other yardstick.

You are yourself and that you are perfectionist in your imperfections.

Confidence doesn't mean having a happy attitude all the time or being shy. It's not about being the most glamorous person at a gathering or having the best friends. It doesn't mean you are without flaws or that you solve each challenge with great effectiveness. Confidence is the feeling of being confident that you are who you are at this moment, in the individual's capabilities, and then working to create the best version of yourself tomorrow. Confidence means embracing every moment and experience without apologies. You might be nervous or loud or say the wrong thing or even not speak at all But ultimately, you're content with yourself.

The feeling of security emanates from a person and other notice it. This is why confident individuals draw others to them. Who wouldn't like to be in a group with such an authentic acceptance of oneself?

Confidence can free you from social anxiety

Someone who is not confident in themselves is hesitant to speak their opinions in a public setting , or even in a social situation. The person is constantly evaluating their thoughts, opinions, their ideas and fears being judged and rejected. A lack of confidence in oneself makes even small talk difficult to carry out. By gaining confidence in yourself You recognize that there is no proper or incorrect way to behave. Your ideas and thoughts are different from those of others. You'll be different from others. You realize that your uniqueness can make you useful to others. You can then be a generous person and have fun in the social setting.

Self-confidence is Not the same as Self-Esteem

Self-confidence and self-esteem can be employed interchangeably, however they are totally different concepts, even though they appear alike. Self-confidence is a term used to describe confidence in one's self, or faith in his own capabilities as well as his judgement and power self-esteem is the assessment of one's worth. "Esteem" originates in the Latin word aestimare which is a reference to "to evaluate. It's not unusual that someone with confidence in themselves but have low self-esteem. This condition is quite common among famous people such as those who kill themselves of drug addiction or even suicide.

Self-confidence varies based on the circumstance However, self-esteem stays fairly constant regardless of the circumstances. A high self-esteem indicates that you place yourself with respect and cherish yourself. In boosting your self-love and self-esteem, you become more confident. A high self-esteem can make you feel happier and less likely to hinder your own success and self-esteem as well as increasing your attraction to other gender!

Here are a few ways to increase your self-esteem

Be aware of how you conduct yourself and speak to yourself. The communication that happens in your own mind is known as intrapersonal communication. You can decide for yourself if it's positive or not. People with low self-esteem tend to be a bit self-critical and interact to themselves in a brutal manner. Be aware of what you tell yourself and the way you conduct yourself. Make sure that your thoughts are empowering instead of putting you down.

Utilize affirmations that are positive to improve the way you think about yourself. A positive affirmation is an emotional positive affirmation. A majority of the things we tell ourselves are a part of our lives to bring about change in your life. One great way to do this is to set a few moments each day examine yourself and say at minimum five positive affirmations about the things you would like to see in your future.

Do not be a comparison with other people. You are a distinct person with your own journey in your life. You'll always be short if you rely on others' standards to gauge your own. Focus on improving your abilities as well as your circumstances and abilities and don't be able to measure your progress against the person you were yesterday.

* You're not perfect. Everyone is not. People with low self-esteem are more likely to believe that they are living up to an unrealistic standard of excellence. You're human. Human beings are human. Learn from these mistakes and move forward.

* Exercise. It is not just an ideal way to connect with others like going into the fitness center or take part in an athletic activity It also increases the amount of hormones, which create a feeling of happiness. These hormones are known as endorphins. They ensure a healthy mental and emotional environment.

• Surround yourself with positive people. Spend less time with negative people who promote the negative image of yourself. It is more likely that you will behave yourself with kindness if you hear positive comments and actions directed at you from the outside.

Also in increasing the amount of areas in your life that you feel confident, you will boost your overall feeling of self-esteem. In most cases, when you work on one aspect, self-confidence or self-esteem in turn, you improve the other. But, it's usually more straightforward to boost self-confidence since it is something you can measure and see. You can track your achievements when you improve your performance in a specific area. For instance, if you are looking to improve your swimmer and improve your confidence in this subject, you could learn classes and do some practice. You can track the progress you make and see your accomplishments come to fruition.

The same applies to the improvement of your socializing and communication abilities. Through practice and commitment, you'll get better at it and increase your confidence in social situations.

Qualities of people who are socially confident

People who are confident in themselves and their ability to perform in social situations have certain characteristics. These characteristics make them easy to recognize. A few of these traits are:

* Being self-aware. Socially confident individuals are honest about themselves. They recognize the strengths as well as weaknesses. They make use of their strengths, while also working to enhance their weaknesses. While socializing, this individual might be skilled in telling stories, but is awkward in maintaining a relaxed posture. The person is able to assess their capabilities and capitalizes on their strengths of storytelling. They also work on improving how they present themselves. They also identify their weaknesses.

* Being honest. A lot of people don't realize the importance of integrity but a confident person knows. Be true to your word. If you have said you're committed to doing something for instance, contact someone, take action. It doesn't matter if you made the commitment for yourself or others, develop your character (and boost your confidence in social situations) by being honest.

* Feel a sense of goal. Drive and motivation are powerful. They provide a person with direction, something to strive towards. With that goal in mind the person will be able to rise from the bed and know precisely what they need to do to achieve their objectives. As we'll discuss later it is crucial to establish goals for conversation and social activities to enable efficient communication. Socially confident people have these goals and will do the things necessary to reach these goals.

* Being gracious. The confident people are able to appreciate the little things they have in their lives and do not hesitate to express gratitude for the tiniest things, like breathing air. This person will never be scared or timid to express gratitude for the company of others or their time.

* Being decisive. This is the hallmark of a leader as well as someone who is often the one to dominate conversations. Many people are scared to make a mistake (such as making a mistake in small conversations) and thus, put off on making

the right choice. But this isn't so for confident people. They can set themselves apart from the rest of the crowd by making choices even the tough ones such as starting small conversation. It could be the incorrect choice, but actions can be taken to rectify the mistake. If you don't make a decision that you are not able to take action, there is no chance of being taken in any way.

* Being assertive. A confident person adheres to their ethics and morals, and isn't unwilling to defend their beliefs or values. A person who is confident isn't a slouch. This translates into how they interact with other people. The person who is like this will attract similar people. Furthermore, since they're open and confident, people are drawn to their leadership even in casual conversation.

* The ability to be funny with themselves. These individuals don't think too much about themselves. They don't sweat the little things and possess a an humour which can help them get through the storm even when clouds are most dark.

They bring this attitude in their conversations and can enhance it by adding humor, if needed.

Tips for Boosting Your SocialSelf-Confidence

The wallflower from the star in the crowd, everybody's social life could benefit from adhering to the guidelines below.

* Begin slow and increase your speed as you progress. If you're not sure about your social abilities, don't take on a large gathering of a thousand people for the first time. It is not putting yourself out of your comfortable zone. You are placing yourself in a position to fail. Start small, for instance, an intimate gathering with close friends at which you can test your conversation skills. Gradually increase your social gatherings. The process of building confidence and trust with your social skills isn't a simple procedure. It's a continuous effort to improve. Don't attempt to skimp steps or you'll fail.

* Schedule your social activities. To build confidence in yourself, you must make the investment of time. You can make use of

the time searching for activities or places that will benefit you the most from the connections you be able to have. For instance, if you are a fan of art, consider attending exhibitions or an artist premier. This is significantly more beneficial the idea of going to a bar for sports in case you don't have any interest in this.

Additionally, by planning your social events in advance you will have time to prepare your mind and also to recite positive affirmations. You can also find relevant information, such as the names of those who will be in attendance before the event. It is possible to find the common interests of people so that you are aware of what subjects you could discuss with the person. This reduces pressure on your mind during the event as there is no need to think up questions to talk about right then and there. This allows you to be free to simply enjoy the events and interactions with the people you meet.

Know what you are doing. Referring to the example of an artist having subjects that you know about will significantly boost your confidence as your brain is stocked with facts and information that are readily available to talk about. Most of the time, you'll discover that you become so immersed in the discussion of these topics that you don't notice feeling nervous or worried.

* Talk, think and be positive. Be aware that negative self-talk is an extremely common thing, and this tendency only gets worse when you are in stressful situations. Be nice to yourself. You can tell yourself that you'll achieve great results and increasing your likelihood of this occurring. In addition, if you promise yourself that you'll confidently interact with others and be responsive to them and others, you will increase the likelihood of doing this. Your mind exerts a significant influence on your body. If you show the confidence you feel within and out, people are drawn towards your positive self.

• Concentrate on the person who you are talking to instead of on you. The study found that those who pay total attention on the person they are speaking to rather then on them feel 70% more relaxed immediately. This is due to the fact that instead on the anxiety you experience and the thoughts the mind is forced to concentrate on the people you are talking to as well as their desires and needs in the conversation instead. Then, you will be able to react appropriately and increase your confidence.

You can fake it until you can make it. Before I get into anything else I'll tell you this: Never attempt to appear to be someone you're not. Be aware that we've already established that you're a special and exceptional person. Actually pretending to be someone else than you in social settings is likely to backfire. But, if you can imitate self-confidence and confidence in social situations you'll be able to imbibe these self-confident traits as time passes.

For this, choose an individual who is confident or a famous person for instance. Take note of their body language as well as the facial expressions they make, and the manner in which they keep eye contact with others. Make sure you behave the same way. If you're in social situations, show these traits that you've learned to do. Even if it is an overwhelming sense of anxiety you'll appear confident in front of people around you and they will react to your confidence. If this is the case more, the less you be required to pretend to be confident and the more comfortable you'll feel.

• Realize that nobody else is as concerned like you. We believe that everyone is watching our shoulders; that others are simply watching, waiting for us be a failure. However, the truth is that in the majority of cases the people around you, particularly strangers, aren't concerned about whether you are winners or losers of any awards in the social realm. The majority of the time, it's just inside your mind. When you are aware of this you can relax and you begin to feel confident within your own skin. This is the true indicator of someone who's completely confident, no matter where they are.

When a person does not possess the confidence required to succeed at a job and is not confident, courage can be a factor. Although you might not have the confidence to become an empathetic social butterfly at the moment, you've got the confidence to attempt and do it even when you are not sure. Courage is a virtue. The ability to be courageous requires you in order to let yourself grow. It opens up possibilities and enhances the capabilities.

As you strive to be assured in every aspect in your daily life, make sure you are confident enough to perform what you have to do during the interim. Therefore, go to that office celebration. Attend that carnival. Visit the reunion of your school. It doesn't matter the location or who is attending simply go. While you are at these events, be sure to communicate with your fellow attendees as best you can to your ability.

Chapter 17: Applying Small Talk To Your Advantage

In the preceding chapters, we examined the ways we can utilize small talk as a way to communicate with our surroundings and expand our social circle. However, small talk is often ignored and people tend to focus on its negatives more than the benefits. Small talk can benefit people in a variety of ways, and help them improve their social skills, both professionally and personally.

This chapter will will look at the many ways you can make use of small talk to enrich your life in numerous ways.

Impressing others

If you can master the art of small talk can make an impressive impression on different people around you. You will be able to impress people with your knowledge and your speaking skills. People will instantly take a impression of your presentation and will judge you to be an excellent speaker. They'll want to engage in conversations with you, and engage in meaningful conversations with you. They'll also make an efforts to get you involved in small discussions and assist you gather new information.

Career building

By engaging in small conversations it will allow you to build relationships. If you begin talking with strangers, some may end up being in the same industry as you, and could be in an even higher level. It is possible to ask for their assistance and advance your career. You can also contact the different people within your organization who are in an extremely influential position, and letting them fall in love with your skills can assist you in building an impressive career. Your confidence in speaking will also attract lots of admirers and allow you to achieve a position of influence with a speedier pace.

Maintain lasting relationships

By having small discussions it is not just possible to be able make new acquaintances and friends, but also keep in touch with your existing ones. It is possible to build lasting relationships by staying in contact with your family and family. If you think about it, idea, it is likely that your current relations started as small discussions and most of them started as a young child. The majority of the conversations you had included fun topics that you enjoyed when you were a kid and talking about it with your friends made it easier to form a solid connection. In the same way, it is important to begin having fun and small talks with them frequently to build a lasting and strong relationship.

Create new ideas

If you get to meet new people, you'll have the opportunity to exchange ideas. You'll be able to learn new concepts and even give some. You'll be able to gain knowledge and use them and enhance your life. You'll expand your horizons and your brain will allow you think more deeply and more insightful thoughts. You'll begin to think more deeply and become extremely knowledgeable and intelligent.

Attention increased

If you engage in small discussions the mind is active. It isn't necessary to be contemplating the same topic for an extended period of time. Moreover, your mind will be attentive to what your partner is talking about. If you are discussing relevant and important things, your mind will remain active. It will be thinking of the things you could respond to. If your brain isn't focused, then you'll start to become lazy while your concentration may be reduced. It's not going to be an issue with conversation.

Problem solution

If you engage in small talk and small talk, you can look at a situation from the other's viewpoint and enable you to tackle a problem with greater speed. You won't have so many disputes and be able to tackle issues using a more systematic method. You'll be able to demonstrate to think critically and develop the capacity to contemplate the viewpoint of the other party's viewpoint and solve various issues.

Growth

You'll begin to observe a growing vocabulary and will notice that you are becoming a little more intelligent. If you are in regular, regular, and regular verbal conversations instead of communicating and receiving messages, you'll start to discover new things. There is a possibility to improve your speaking as well as see an increase in your ability to contribute positive value to conversations.

Overall development

By engaging in little talk, you'll be able to develop your personality. You'll be able to talk more easily and be able to interact with people with confidence. You won't have the difficulty of not having a subject to talk about since you are familiar of the most recent happenings and news stories and be able to talk about them with confidence.

Inspire

If you begin to have a chat with your loved ones and your family and let them witness the positive effect you are having on yourself You will encourage them to follow suit. With new confidence and motivation they will begin to put the small-talking routine into action. They will be grateful to you for inspiring them and , together, you'll begin to see an improvement in your outlook.

Cross cultural chasms

By engaging in conversation it is possible to bridge the cultural gap. It is possible to meet people from different religious and cultural backgrounds and, as a result, you will learn about their customs and lifestyles. When you engage in small conversations with other people who speak a different language, you are able to learn a completely new language and gain enormous benefits from this activity.

Chapter 18: Listening With Care

As we said, having the term "good conversational skills" does not just refer to the ability to speak to others. It also involves listening with attention. Since conversations are an ongoing process that involves two parties It is crucial that people know how to listen learn how to communicate as well as master the art of smaller talking. This chapter will guide you through some of the techniques that can help you improve your listening abilities.

The ability to listen is crucial as people use it throughout their lives. Students require excellent listening skills to be attentive to the lessons the teacher teaches in class. Students need to be able to listen when their parents give them tips. You will require good hearing skills when your manager wants you to finish a task. Below are a few of the suggestions that can assist you in developing and maintaining the ability to listen:

Concentrate your attention. When you're speaking to others be sure your focus is on your audience. Be sure to keep your distractions at bay. Avoid doing things that are unnecessary since this could prevent you from paying attention. If you let yourself get distracted by other things then you'll be unable to comprehend the words spoken by the speaker. If you are distracted, you could discover yourself repeatedly asking what the person has spoken about. This isn't a sign of good communication skills.

Take note of the most important phrases. If someone is speaking at you, don't need to know the exact words the person is saying. There is a way to comprehend what the speaker is saying, without having the exact words they are employing. One method to figure out the meaning of what the speaker is talking about is to take out the words that are used in the sentence. Keywords are important words which define the meaning or significance of a phrase or sentence. For instance, a speaker may say "I was at the store yesterday to buy some meat." The main keywords are supermarket purchase, yesterday, and meat. These words alone will ensure that you can understand the speaker even if aren't sure how they've said these words.

Repeat. Some sentences and words even if they are clearly stated cannot be properly understood. This is why it is imperative to take the time to repeat what you believe you received by reciting what the person speaking stated. If you do this you'll be able clarify what the speaker is saying. This will help you avoid confusion. But, it's not required to say precisely what the speaker stated. It is better to rephrase the message and then say it the way you can comprehend the meaning. By doing this you will allow the speaker to be capable of correcting you in case you didn't understand what he or was trying to convey.

Be aware of non-verbal communication. Listening is not just the ability to listen to how the speech is being said. It also includes the ability to discern the non-verbal methods of communication the speaker projects. For instance, when two of you are talking to one another but suddenly he or she slumps. This could indicate that they are already disinterested and bored. By being able to discern non-verbal signals someone is indicating then you'll be able to react appropriately. For instance, you might come up with a better topic to discuss or enhance your voice to make it more lively.

Don't interrupt. Give the speaker time to complete what he or she is saying before commenting or make a comment. If you react abruptly when the speaker is speaking, you will not be able to hear what the speaker is actually talking about. You'll only be able to understand only a portion of what they are saying but not the whole. This can lead to confusion due to the fact that you didn't let them to complete their thoughts. There may be other thoughts and messages would like to communicate however you weren't in a position to comprehend them as you had already interrupted. Be sure to ensure that the speaker is finished first. This is also a gesture of respect and politeness.

Pay pay attention on the sound. The tone of the words aren't the only indication that tell you what the person speaking wants to convey. In most cases the tone of his voice is crucial. When you are able to discern the different tones of their voice, you'll be able distinguish between a mood and another. It is easy to tell if the person speaking is happy, angry or sad, and dissatisfied by listening carefully at the sound of their voice.

These are just a few of the suggestions and reminders to aid you in improving your listening abilities. It is important to be aware that conversations are one-way communication. You will never be able to master conversational skills if you aren't able to listen well.

Chapter 19: Take The Plunge

Get out and take the leap! There's no chance of meeting people who aren't within your own corner.

Find out the places where the people are!

Create a Positive First Impression using Nonverbal Clues

People are usually quick to judge based on just simply looking at the appearance an individual. You are one the majority? What are the times you make assumptions about someone else due to their appearance or dress or behave?

You could be among those who insist that you do not make judgments until you've got to know someone else. It is human nature to make judgments about others at the first time of meeting.

Here are some easy ways to help you make the best impression before you begin to talk:

Technique #3 Show Enthusiasm

Feel full of joy and enthusiasm. Studies have shown that it's easy for anyone to alter their mood. You can make an effort to be happier and cheerful. As with many people, you fail to recognize that you are able to be more in control of your emotions and feelings more that you thought.

If people can see that you are happy and positive outlook people will view that you are friendly and optimistic. This will, in turn receive a positive reaction from them. Be genuinely joyful and cheerful Your body language will reflect your mood. Be positive, encouraging and friendly and you'll make people feel comfortable around your.

Technique #4 Maintain Upright Posture

Your posture can be an indicator of the way you feel at the moment. Be conscious of your posture, particularly when you're getting ready for an interaction. Be conscious of what you are going to communicate and also how you move your body.

Take a pen and piece of paper. note at least five traits you would like others to notice and feel when speaking with you:

Be confident

Enthusiastic

Open

Bold

The most comfortable

After you've completed the list, try to think of one person who embodies all the characters mentioned above. After you've finished, imagine the person. Look at how they stand and how they move.

Practice their moves before the mirror. Is your posture straight? Are your shoulders at the correct position or do they seem to be sagging? As you work, notice the way you feel. Straight-up stance is the ideal posture to aim for.

Your posture improves confidence.

Technique #5 Make Eye Contact

There's nothing more difficult than trying to communicate with one who is always fiddling on their cell phone while they talk to you. Someone who seems to be listening , but does not even look you in the eyes.

Eye contact is a straightforward method of making relationships with others. If someone is looking away when talking towards you, that means that the person isn't really interested in the conversation.

Technique #6 Dress to Impress.

It doesn't mean you have to dress in designer clothing. It is not necessary to spend money on expensive clothes and accessories in order to make an impression. You can continue to wear your existing clothes.

It is the way you present yourself before people which is the most important thing.

Dressing for the occasion is also a sign that you don't have to dress in fancy attire and costly accessories. It's how you present your self that makes your mark.

Breaking the Ice

The beginning is always toughest. It is often a struggle for most people to start an exchange of words, particularly when you're meeting on the first occasion. What are the best ways to start a conversation?

It's normal to feel anxious when trying to start the conversation with a stranger. Once you have overcome that fear, you'll be prepared.

Technique #7 Use Your Surroundings

It's always easier for people to make use of their surroundings. Engage in an exchange about something you have seen while walking to the event or share an anecdote you're aware about.

If you're going to an event an event, seminar, or gathering, you must always make use of the surrounding.

It could be like this "Are you from the area? I'm sure I haven't met previously."

Perhaps you're at a party to welcome an incoming employee to the business. It is possible to start conversations with them with this question: "Where are you from?" Then proceed by asking them how they have enjoyed the experience to date.

The only thing you have to do is explore and be inventive.

Technique #8 Use Current Events

Keep in mind that you could always discuss current events to spark conversation. The current events are reliable. Always be prepared. Make sure you take at minimum a few minutes to reading the headlines of the paper or watch the news on TV or look for news via an online news website.

The idea is to utilize something that everybody is comfortable with. You'll be amazed by what other people's reactions to it. Everybody has opinions regarding the current situation of the country. Everybody has an opinion.

Practice #9: ask questions. wait for answers.

You are happy when someone asks questions and waits patiently to hear your answer. It is always satisfying when you know someone has an keen interest in your thoughts.

The most effective way to obtain interesting responses from another person is to pose open-ended questions. If you ask questions that are answerable with either yes or no, and you'll not get any answers.

Pay attention to the other person's response.

A question that is open-ended can be described like this "How did the game go?" You will get an endless stream of updates on what happened during the game instead of asking "Did you take home the victory?" , which will result in an answer of "yes" or "no."

Technique #10 Just Say Hello

Sometimes, it's the simplest things that can trigger a huge response. It's not always necessary to think of new ways to begin conversations. Simply saying "Hello!" makes all the difference. Make sure to follow up by saying your name.

Another person can become comfortable and will end up the person giving their name immediately.

What's wrong with trying to say hello to anyone who passes by? After you have your coffee in the morning and you're at the cafe, greet security personnel at the entrance.

Technique #11 Give Genuine Compliments

A compliment is a good method of breaking the ice. However, the compliment needs to be genuine. Don't give it simply because.

If for example, you see yourself sitting next to an expert at the table for lunch

You can inform the speaker that the talk was great. Be sure to only mention that if you actually listened to the talk and enjoyed it.

However in the event that you don't discover something interesting in the lecture or presentation, you can tell the speaker, "Thank you for taking time to share your experience."

If you are unable to find something you like You can look into other methods.

Technique #12 Ask for Opinions

Get the conversation started by asking the opinion of another person. If you're working on a project and you're concerned about whether you're performing it correctly. You could ask a friend to help you, "Can I take a couple of minutes? Would you like to check this book out. Let me know what you think of it."

This is a great opportunity to initiate the conversation. Many people feel gratified knowing that someone needed assistance.

Being genuine is essential to the quality of your relationships. Whatever you do to attempt to begin conversations If you're not authentic you will appear in a way that is fake or forced.

Feeling uncomfortable when you meet strangers will end up creating a massive barrier in between yourself and world outside. It's high time to make a change.

Find out what you're afraid of. Here are some examples:

Are you afraid rejection?

Are you worried about saying something foolish?

Are you afraid to fail?

Do you have doubts about your abilities and capabilities?

This fear should be put to rest now.

If you're concerned that you don't have anything interesting to say, you can spend some time searching for topics to discuss. Learn more about the topic or watch documentaries to stay up-to-date with the latest news. However in case you're scared of rejection, you do not need to be worried. If you're rejected simply take it as an opportunity to improve your skills and attempt to do it again.

Chapter 20: The Openings that Are Suitable for People who are shy

You may want to listen more instead of talking. It's perfectly normal. If you are thinking of the kinds of things you'd like to know about someoneelse, it's easy to pass the microphone over to them, asking them questions that let them do all the talking. People like to share their personal stories and so let them speak about what they would like to do most. In the meantime you'll be able listen and discover more about them and determine how they fit in your life the way you would like to.

These are some topics which provide plenty of discussion. They require a lot of thought, and give the opportunity to continue the discussion with questions to follow up.

"If you were given the option of all jobs around the globe, which would you pick?"

It's a good question since the person you're speaking to has to dig deeper for answers. You might be amazed by the answers they give and could help you get to know them better than if you were to engage with them using the standard "chat up" phrases like "what's happening" or "how do you feel." Conversations isn't going to be over quickly and the person you are talking to will be delighted to be there with you. Another benefit of asking these questions is that they place yourself in a situation where the whole conversation is relevant and not "just conversational."

Another great way to break the ice would be:

"What is it that you are passionate about?"

The kind of question that you ask requires a bit of a preface or a conversation leading to the question, particularly if it is being asked to someone who is completely unfamiliar. I usually lead the discussion by explaining why I'm undertaking a social test to find out what people take satisfaction in, typically and accompanied by smiles. When you make this statement to the person in front of you, making them feel less secure because they are forced to answer such a huge question. This will make people more likely to give the answer to keep the conversation moving forward. My experience has shown that people are extremely helpful in answering , and they may spend a moment to do some reflection before responding. The most appealing aspect of this type of question can be that it allows you to be able to enter to an area that you both enjoy and get the two of you thinking about something essential to you both.

These are just a few examples of how you can guide the conversation to where you're looking for it to take it. The most important thing to be careful about is avoiding questions that are only requiring quick, yes or zero answers in the least amount possible. Sure, there are certain to be some however, the emphasis is on asking questions that provide both you as well as the other person value. Rememberthat they is going to be evaluating you also, so make sure that your questions worth asking.

Here are some other worth-while questions to start with:

"What's your ideal luxury vacation?"

"Where is your mind going prior to going to bed at the end of the night?"

"What's the most bizarre thing that's has ever happened in your life?"

I'm also adding an article which includes 48 queries to make the discussion lively and interesting on this site:

It is possible to make your conversation more meaningful for both of you, and yet remain true to your authentic self. You'll start conversations that don't offend or bore you. Moreover, it's likely to be an unidirectional conversation that makes it much easier to navigate. It also shows your friend that you're an individual who is a person of depth and is willing to listen. This is essential for all human beings, so it puts you in a great position to establish a connection.

Don't forget, attempting to approach an encounter in a sloppy way could leave you feeling trapped in the conversation or arrive at a point that the conversation stalls. This is likely to confirm your dislike for small talk , and may even make you feel more absorbed. If you introduce questions that prompt someone else to speak with you, you will learn more about them by simply watching. Be aware that you might have to make small nods in appropriate places to encourage the other person to go forward with things such as "and ..." or "and what else?" or just a physical smile.

What you're doing is giving the initiative to the person in question as you would say, "Please carry on". It could be that you're permitting the person to speak at times which will allow them to be more genuine and inclined to establish a connection with you. You can use a powerful tool to use small conversations for your benefit. Keep in mind that you might be asked questions too so be prepared with your story. Don't worry, when you are in the mood to do so, you are able to change the subject by asking a question that could put the other person in the spotlight once more. For instance, you can declare "I am able to talk about my life for hours. I'm curious about what's going on with your life." This automatically places you in a advantageous position since people aren't used to having this kind of freedom in conversation, and they you will be pleasantly surprised. It is also possible to use facial expressions such as eye contact, facial expressions and body language to demonstrate that you are truly paying attention to what the person says. Eye contact is essential since they are trying to get your approval. Keep eye contact and look at your eyes whenever something they say hits just the right notes. Smiles with your eyes will convey more than words. You will also discover it to be much more easy to achieve rather than trying to be authentic by what you speak. Allow them to listen to your thoughts through your body language, as you don't need to speak much about anything, which is an additional benefit for you my fellow introverts. You'll have an advantage over the people who engage with small talk as an usual routine thing to do. The person you're listening to would like to hear from you, therefore please them. Perhaps they'll start to build the relationship, not you.

Chapter 21: Display Genuine Interest

A genuine interest in the people you're talking to, regardless of the person they are, is crucial when it comes down to conversation. This is the single step that can transform you from being a decent small talker into an outstanding one. You might even be referred to by people you as a true "people person" when you master this skill.

One of the most lovely ladies I've ever had the pleasure of meeting was a teacher at school. I had a chat with her on a set for a film one time because we were working with her daughter for commercial. The lady was (and I'll repeat) among the most pleasant people I've ever met. We probably talked for about 30 minutes but I didn't see her again.

Thirty. Minutes.

I really believed it was possible to trust her with my most tense and secrets. It was possible to call her at any time and ask her to a coffee shop and she'd say yes.

How did this woman make such an impression on me in such a an incredibly short time?

The reason to that is she seemed truly fascinated by all I said. Every word that was spoken by me she responded with excitement and interest. These two aspects are the key to successful small-talking. If you can master these two elements then you can be able to master small-talk.

Enthusiasm

The definition of "enthusiasm" is an intense and enthusiastic joy or interest.

What does it mean to be passionate and excited? If you're having a conversation with someone you've never met the most effective and quickest method to earn the trust of them is to display enthusiasm. This is basically exaggerated joy at what they say. However, this doesn't mean that you're acting "fake" however, rather contrary.

This means that you truly would like to know more about their experience and that you will not criticize them regardless of what they have to say. You react positively and enthusiastically to anything they say because you're eager to learn more.

"Wow you water ski? It's so cool! I'd be way too scared to try this."

"Omg this is your puppy"? He's adorable! I'd love to have an animal like him."

"You are addicted to cocaine on a regular basis? Wow! You must be a party maniac What kind of music do you like to listen to?"

The reason why engage in a spirited response to what they're saying is that you're subconsciously communicating two things to them:

They entertain you by what they are telling you. It makes them feel happy.

You like these.

The second is the most crucial one. When human beings are placed in situations in which they might feel uncomfortable, the main thing they would like to be is to be accepted. To be accepted, other participants in the room should agree with them. What you do when you respond with enthusiasm to their stories is you're telling them you're awestruck by them.

If they mention something personal, such as "I really enjoy playing games on my PC" You respond by saying "oh Wow, that's so nerdy." You're not a fan and end any relationship you could have made with the person. You've lost their trust, and they'll be less likely to tell you about things, and less likely to to become your friend.

You would like the person with whom you're talking in confidence. This can help establish a relationship that could last during the course of your conversation or the length of your friendship.

I'd like to use this opportunity to make sure that I am clear on the subject matter. Being authentic means the person you're dealing with is honest, and honest. If you like the person or react enthusiastically to them however, it doesn't mean that you need to be in agreement with what they've said. The most important thing you don't would like to do in conversation with a stranger is to appear fake. If they don't see through you in the beginning they'll be able to see through you once you become friends. The point to talk about small things is to build a connection that may last beyond that particular party, one date or networking event.

Approval implies that you do not condemn or judge them, but however, it doesn't mean that you are in agreement with all of them. If they tell you that they drink a lot of cocaine every weekend, you reply in a manner that is honest, such as: "oh wow that sounds absurd, but I'm not sure I can do that, I'm too straight." Being open and sharing your thoughts in a respectful manner can be a good method to begin moving the conversation away from tinny conversations and towards something deeper.

I'm sure I mentioned facial expressions in my final chapter However, body language can be an amazing way to display enthusiasm. Utilizing gestures and facial expressions even exaggerated ones , is a great method to motivate the other person to continue talking.

Have you ever engaged in conversation with someone who you realized wasn't listening you? It's a pain. It's endless and the person is contemplating something else or checking their phone. You realize that you're not making any progress with the person. The emotion you're experiencing in this moment is one of disapproval. Always try that the one speaking to you feel comfortable. If you are able to do this and on a higher scale (ie. laughter at jokes) the higher they will view your character.

If you're enjoying their jokes and expressing their opinions, the more they'll think "wow that person (or woman) was such a nice person. I had a blast having conversations with them."

Intrigue

Another aspect that made this lady wonderful and pleasant to chat with was the fact that she displayed interest. She was eager to know more about everything I discussed and yes, they all. When I mentioned that I enjoyed mountain biking, she'd inquire about it as if she wanted to try mountain biking for herself.

Imagine that your favorite thing on earth is knitting. You're a voracious knitter. You tell me that you love knitting, and I pretend as if I would like to try it myself. I ask questions like:

Wow, that's amazing!What kinds of things do you create?

Do you find it difficult to master or did you take several years?

What's a simple thing to knit that an beginner can learn?

These questions show an interest in your favorite subject. You'll be talking about the best way to knit , and even when I don't really care anything about knitting however, the conversation is making you feel very content.

Following up questions tell who you'd like to know more details about what they're telling you. It's like you're telling them "wow you're fascinating Tell me more about yourself I'm interested to know more about you". This is the most flattering compliment that a human could give to someone else.

Conclusion

Learning to initiate small conversations isn't difficult if you dedicate your time and energy to it. It's all you need to do is be willing to learn the art of small talk. Also, you must be willing to make connections with people befriend them and find out more about them simply by speaking to them about minor, light and positive subjects.

I hope this book given you the tools to start small conversations. These tips are simple to follow and apply. So, you won't be unable to use these tips the next time you want to meet someone to chat about things.

The great thing about learning to talk in small groups is that it can be crucial to achieving larger goals, and that means improving your communication, conversation and social abilities. In this way you'll be able to talk to people in a more calm and more confident way and thus expanding your circle of friends and networks.

www.ingramcontent.com/pod-product-compliance
Lightning Source LLC
Chambersburg PA
CBHW071839080526
44589CB00012B/1049